"When it comes to reading the Bible with my kids, I am among the well-meaning and terrified. I find that I don't know where to start or how to navigate past my own faith baggage to engage my kids in healthy, wonder-filled conversations about God's story. This Bible devotional offers a way in. It honors questions, engages creativity, and is flexible enough to work for your particular family, no matter where you're at. What a gift!"

ADDIE ZIERMAN, author of *When We Were on Fire* and *Night Driving*

"*The Family Bible Devotional* is a great resource for parents who want to engage their children in fresh and meaningful discussions about the Bible as they explore stories and passages together. Fun activities, interesting facts, and thought-provoking questions will turn family devotions from boring to exciting. I wish I had this book when my kids were growing up!"

CRYSTAL BOWMAN, best-selling, award-winning author of over 100 books for children, including *Our Daily Bread for Kids*

"*The Family Bible Devotional* has added a fresh new dimension to mornings with my 13-year-old daughter. Background information, Scripture unhampered by verse notations (it reads like a story!), and thought-provoking questions and prayer prompts not only serve to structure our discussions during busy breakfast time, but challenge us to consider Scripture from new perspectives. My daughter has been inspired to ask tough questions and deepen her understanding of the Bible, all before the school bus comes around the corner!"

TANIA RUNYAN, poet and author of *How to Write a Poem*, *How to Read a Poem*, and *How to Write a College Application Essay*

"In this excellent devotional, Sarah Wells has packed a lifetime of inspiration and joyful applications that will guide families into a deeper appreciation of Scripture."

DANDI DALEY MACKALL, award-winning author of over 500 books for adults and children, including *My Bible Animals Storybook*

"When writing for children, especially when topics are confusing or tough to wade through, I think it's important for kids to have a narrator they can trust, and Wells doesn't disappoint. Her writing is friendly and thought-provoking, and the activities she's designed to go along with the devotions are creative and fun. Here's a family devotional that allows parents to walk alongside their children as they explore God's story, and find their place in it."

CALLIE FEYEN, author of *Romeo & Juliet: The Teacher Diaries*

"This book is truly a gift: fun, creative, and sound. My family loved it!"

CRAIG HOVEY, author of *Unexpected Jesus: The Gospel as Surprise* and *To Share in the Body: A Theology of Martyrdom for Today's Church*

"A love of Scripture is something that is taught. Sarah Wells has created a tool that can help parents do just that for our children. Thanks, Sarah, for writing such a great resource for families!"

STEVEN COLE, Executive Director, The Brethren Church Denomination

"Trying to engage the whole family in Bible study in a way that feels authentic and beneficial often leaves me feeling lost. But Sarah Wells is a trustworthy guide. *The Family Bible Devotional* makes Scripture accessible and memorable. My kids kept bringing up the stories they'd heard in this devotional for days after we read them—and I learned new things, too."

AMY PETERSON, author of *Dangerous Territory: My Misguided Quest to Save the World* and contributor to *Our Daily Bread*

"I like it a lot!"

ROSIE, age 9, who kept reading the book on her own after family devotions were done

The FAMILY BIBLE DEVOTIONAL

STORIES FROM THE BIBLE TO HELP KIDS & PARENTS ENGAGE & LOVE SCRIPTURE

SARAH M. WELLS

Our Daily Bread Publishing™

The Family Bible Devotional: Stories from the Bible to Help Kids and Parents Engage and Love Scripture
© 2018 by Discovery House (Our Daily Bread Publishing)

ISBN: 978-1-62707-886-3

Library of Congress Cataloging-in-Publication Data
Names: Wells, Sarah M., author.
Title: The family Bible devotional : stories from the Bible to help kids and parents engage and love scripture / Sarah M. Wells.
Description: Grand Rapids : Discovery House, 2018. | Includes bibliographical references.
Identifiers: LCCN 2018011006 | ISBN 9781627078863 (pbk.)
Subjects: LCSH: Bible stories, English. | Bible—Miscellanea. | Families—Religious life.
Classification: LCC BS550.3 .W455 2018 | DDC 220.95/05—dc23
LC record available at https://lccn.loc.gov/2018011006

Printed in the United States of America
20 21 22 23 24 25 26 / 8 7 6 5 4 3 2

Contents

Introduction

"Scripture is like a river again, broad and deep, shallow enough here for the lamb to go wading, but deep enough there for the elephant to swim."

—Saint Gregory the Great, *Commentary on the Blessed Book of Job*, written between 578 and 595 AD

This family devotional aims to cultivate healthy conversation between parents and their children about the Bible and its stories. The Bible is a challenging text, woven together and written with intention, to help us find meaning and understand the world in which we live through the lens of faith. Through God, the Bible writers sought to make faith relevant for the next generation. Not just so that faith wouldn't fizzle out and become irrelevant, but because they found their understanding of who God is and how God relates to people so important and meaningful that they could not imagine letting their story—our story—end.

Even though the Bible as we know it hasn't had any new books added to it or removed from it in the last sixteen hundred years or so, we are a part of its ongoing tale of faith and relationship with God, who continues to reveal himself in powerful ways through the Holy Spirit.

We are a part of God's unfolding story, a magnificent story that begins ages and ages before the chapter we're in right now. To see ourselves as part of God's story means that we must also know what precedes us in this narrative. What is our faith's history? How have people pursued God in the past? How can we know who he is and what he values? Should we make it up as we go along, or should we benefit from thousands of years of study, thought, consideration, and prayer to arrive cushioned by the labor of men and women who have come before us?

We're about to explore with our children stories that show us how we can engage with God. The Bible has endured centuries of criticism, wear and tear, translation, oral tradition, transcription, condemnation, misinterpretation, abuse, and praise. It is worthy of wrestling with. It can handle our poking and prodding, our questioning and doubting. It is filled with imperfect people who yelled at God, denied God, cried out for God, wrestled with God, and crucified God, and yet God was ever patient, ever merciful, and ever present with his unfailing love, forgiveness, and acceptance.

As a parent myself, I want my children to know and understand God's Word (as best as it can be understood). I want them to have answers for the hope that they have. But I also want to empower them to ask questions. This life is hard. I don't have all of the answers. You don't have all of the answers. But that doesn't mean we shouldn't dig into the hard questions. What safer place to do that than around the dinner table with your parents? What safer place to humble ourselves than with our spouses and children, admitting we sometimes just don't know?

The questions in this devotional are intended to spark conversation about and to develop a knowledge base of the biblical stories that form the narrative of our faith. I suspect that by exploring these passages with your children, you might find yourself challenged anew by *their* questions, and perhaps even humbled back to the reality of God's God-ness and our human-ness. My hope is that these devotionals will be a companion on your family's faith journey.

Tips to Keep the Kids Engaged

I practiced each of these devotions with my three children, ages six, ten, and eleven, mostly around the dinner table while we were waiting for the kids (particularly the youngest, slowest eater) to finish their meals. I learned a thing or two about how to prevent my kids from hating this time (and made some drastic revisions to the first draft because of this!):

1. **Don't read *to* your kids; read *with* your kids.** Invite your children (even the youngest ones) to take turns reading the Bible passages. This will help them focus on the Bible stories. I chose to include full psalms in some places because these poems are some of the most powerful examples of how God listens to the full spectrum of the human heart, even the parts that make us uncomfortable.

2. **Skip things.** If your kids don't respond well to a question, move on. Judge your children's attention spans each time and adjust your expectations for what they can handle. You want them to engage and love Scripture, not reject and dread reading it.

3. **But don't skip the activities.** I'll be honest—the activities were my least favorite thing to write. I am not a crafty craftsman. I *live* for words. But my kids? They love active learning. This is where the rubber meets the road. Pairing the Bible passages with the activities will help them see how the words of the Bible are active and present in their lives.

4. **Move at your own pace.** Sometimes we read devotionals a few nights in a row and other times, because of sports practices and dinner commitments and bad attitudes, we waited a week and a half before getting back into the material. Make space for reading together, but allow yourselves freedom to deviate from that routine when needed.

5. **Have fun!** Crazy things happen in the Bible. Allow for some craziness, some bold questions, and some honesty about this crazy sacred text of ours. That honesty can crack open our hardened hearts and make us more vulnerable, authentic followers of Christ. "For the word of God is alive and active. Sharper than any double-edged sword, it penetrates even to dividing soul and spirit, joints and marrow; it judges the thoughts and attitudes of the heart" (Hebrews 4:12 NIV).

And God Said
It Was Good

SETTING UP THE STORY

The stories in Genesis were originally passed down from parents to children by a thing called *oral tradition*. The stories that were told were shared in ways that helped people memorize them and repeat them so they could be shared again with future generations. You might notice that some stories in Genesis sound like poems or short stories. Stories like the first one in the Bible help us understand our relationship to God and to the world.

READ: GENESIS 1 (NIV)

In the beginning God created the heavens and the earth. Now the earth was formless and empty, darkness was over the surface of the deep, and the Spirit of God was hovering over the waters.

And God said, "Let there be light," and there was light. God saw that the light was good, and he separated the light from the darkness. God called the light "day," and the darkness he called "night." And there was evening, and there was morning—the first day.

And God said, "Let there be a vault between the waters to separate water from water." So God made the vault and separated the water under the vault from the water above it. And it was so. God called the vault "sky." And there was evening, and there was morning—the second day.

And God said, "Let the water under the sky be gathered to one place, and let dry ground appear." And it was so. God called the dry ground "land," and the gathered waters he called "seas." And God saw that it was good.

Then God said, "Let the land produce vegetation: seed-bearing plants and trees on the land that bear fruit with seed in it, according to their various kinds." And it was so. The land produced vegetation: plants bearing seed according to their kinds and trees bearing fruit with seed in it according to their kinds. And God saw that it was good. And there was evening, and there was morning—the third day.

And God said, "Let there be lights in the vault of the sky to separate the day from the night, and let them serve as signs to mark sacred times, and days and years, and let them be lights in the vault of the sky to give light on the earth." And it was so. God made two great lights—the greater light to govern the day and the lesser light to govern the night. He also made the stars. God set them in the vault of the sky to give light on the earth, to govern the day and the night, and to separate light from darkness. And God saw that it was good. And there was evening, and there was morning—the fourth day.

And God said, "Let the water teem with living creatures, and let birds fly above the earth across the vault of the sky." So God created the great creatures of the sea and every living thing with which the water teems and that moves about in it, according to their kinds, and every winged bird according to its kind. And God saw that it was good. God blessed them and said, "Be fruitful and increase in number and fill the water in the seas, and let the birds increase on the earth." And there was evening, and there was morning—the fifth day.

And God said, "Let the land produce living creatures according to their kinds: the livestock, the creatures that move along the ground, and the wild animals, each according to its kind." And it was so. God made the wild animals according to their kinds, the livestock according to their kinds, and all the creatures that move along the ground according to their kinds. And God saw that it was good.

Then God said, "Let us make mankind in our image, in our likeness, so that they may rule over the fish in the sea and the birds in the sky, over the livestock and all the wild animals, and over all the creatures that move along the ground."

So God created mankind in his own image,

in the image of God he created them;
male and female he created them.

God blessed them and said to them, "Be fruitful and increase in number; fill the earth and subdue it. Rule over the fish in the sea and the birds in the sky and over every living creature that moves on the ground."

Then God said, "I give you every seed-bearing plant on the face of the whole earth and every tree that has fruit with seed in it. They will be yours for food. And to all the beasts of the earth and all the birds in the sky and all the creatures that move along the ground—everything that has the breath of life in it—I give every green plant for food." And it was so.

God saw all that he had made, and it was very good. And there was evening, and there was morning—the sixth day.

TALK ABOUT IT

- What are some patterns you hear when you read this story?
- What do those patterns tell you about God and the creation of the world?
- When God creates people, how are they described? What jobs does God give them?
- What do you think it means to be "made in God's image"? How does it make you feel?
- Is there anything that confuses you about this first story? If so, it's okay! Do you have any questions about Genesis 1? It's time to ask your questions about the Bible.

Parents: During each family devotional, there will be the opportunity for asking questions—the parents get to ask questions, and the kids get to ask questions too. If you don't know the answer, it's okay to say so. As parents, we can empower our children to ask questions about God and the Bible. This curiosity and freedom will pave the way for a meaningful and healthy relationship with God as they grow into adults.

Be willing to share your own questions about God or this particular story during this time. Sharing our own journeys of faith with our kids will help them see how you can have doubts and fears and still love God and be loved by God.

CLOSING THOUGHT

The first chapter of Genesis sets the scene for all of the Bible. It establishes God as the boss. He is the author of the story of creation, from the first burst of energy in the universe to this very second—and beyond! Notice how everything God creates he calls "good." The sun and the moon and the stars, the light and the dark, the water and the air and the land, the plants and the animals—all good, good, good. Everything God created is good because God is good!

In a later part of the Bible, one of God's followers, Paul, says in Philippians 1:6 that God is going to keep on doing the good work in us and on earth until we're a finished product, fine-tuned and complete. In this way, the creation story described in Genesis 1 doesn't end. It's still happening, in you and in me and in the world all around us.

PRAYER PROMPT

If God called all of creation "good," then we can too! As we pray together tonight, let's name off some of the things God created that we're thankful for, that make us laugh or feel amazed. Everything in the universe reflects the good work that God has done and continues to do. Let's pray together Psalm 148, in which the songwriter calls upon creation to praise God too.

ACTIVITY #1: TAKE A HIKE!

Get outdoors and explore! What do you see around you that God made? What do you smell? What do you hear? What is it about creation that you love? What do you see that you are grateful for?

ACTIVITY #2: I SPY, A TO Z

Can you name one thing God made for each letter of the alphabet? Put your minds together to see what crazy things in nature you can name that God made.

Creation Stories

Other tribes and cultures all around the world have their own creation stories like Genesis. Even though the stories vary from culture to culture, it seems as if God wrote into our DNA a desire to understand where we came from and what it is we're doing here. People all around the globe are seeking meaning in life. We can be grateful that God revealed himself through Jesus Christ so that people everywhere can have access to a better understanding of who God is and how he relates to us.

The Word and the Light

SETTING UP THE STORY

Did you know that there is another creation story in the Bible? It happens in one of the books that talks about Jesus. It is the book of John. In *that* creation story, John tells us that Jesus (John calls Jesus "the Word") was God and was with God in the beginning, creating right alongside him! Some people think that's why the Genesis story says, "let *us* create mankind in *our* image," because of the way that God the Father and God the Son and God the Holy Spirit were working together to create everything, including men and women. Let's read John 1 to see how "the Word" and the last story we read connect.

READ: JOHN 1:1–18 (NLT)

In the beginning the Word already existed.

The Word was with God,

and the Word was God.

He existed in the beginning with God.

God created everything through him,

and nothing was created except through him.

The Word gave life to everything that was created,

and his life brought light to everyone.

The light shines in the darkness,

and the darkness can never extinguish it.

God sent a man, John the Baptist, to tell about the light so that everyone might believe because of his testimony. John himself was not the light; he was simply a witness to tell about the light. The one who is the true light, who gives light to everyone, was coming into the world.

He came into the very world he created, but the world didn't recognize him. He came to his own people, and even they rejected him. But to all who believed him and accepted him, he gave the right to become children of God. They are reborn—not with a physical birth resulting from human passion or plan, but a birth that comes from God.

So the Word became human and made his home among us. He was full of unfailing love and faithfulness. And we have seen his glory, the glory of the Father's one and only Son.

John testified about him when he shouted to the crowds, "This is the one I was talking about when I said, 'Someone is coming after me who is far greater than I am, for he existed long before me.'"

From his abundance we have all received one gracious blessing after another. For the law was given through Moses, but God's unfailing love and faithfulness came through Jesus Christ. No one has ever seen God. But the unique One, who is himself God, is near to the Father's heart. He has revealed God to us.

TALK ABOUT IT

- What do you learn about Jesus (or The Word) from these verses?
- How do you think Genesis 1 and John 1 are connected? (Flip to pages 13–15 if you want to reread Genesis 1.)
- Who was John and what was his job?
- What does this passage say about why Jesus came?
- There is a lot of figurative language in this introduction to Jesus. Do any of the sayings confuse you? If so, it's okay! Do you have any questions about John 1? It's time to ask your questions about the Bible.

CLOSING THOUGHT

In Genesis 1 we saw how God created everything, and everything God created was good. In John 1, God reveals even more of himself through his Son, Jesus. Because Jesus is the light of the world, we can travel through our lives with his light guiding us, showing us faith, hope, and love, even in the darkest times.

As we continue to study the Bible, we'll do so with Jesus-colored glasses, remembering that the Word (Jesus) was with God in the beginning, creating right alongside him. With those Jesus-colored glasses, the whole Bible—and the whole world—is illuminated with the true light that gives light! Through Jesus Christ and the Holy Spirit, we can find meaning and light in a world of darkness.

PRAYER PROMPT

The passage we read today talked about the light shining in the darkness and how the darkness has not overcome it. Sometimes it feels as if the darkness in our world overpowers the good. Let's pray today that God would show us his light, his hope, and his peace, even when things feel hopeless, dark, and scary. You might also pray together Psalm 23, one of the most beloved poems in the Bible. God's light triumphs over darkness and will never leave us.

ACTIVITY: SHINE A LITTLE LIGHT

Have your parents help you gather a candle and a match and come together in one room of your house. Draw the shades and turn off lamps until the room is as dark as you can make it, then light the candle. How did the darkness make you feel? What happened to the darkness when the candle was lit? How did the light make you feel? Talk about how God is described as the light of the world, the true light that gives light, and think some more about what that means for us.

Two Johns!

Just like today, there are sometimes people in the Bible who have similar or the same first names. The author of the book of John was one of Jesus's twelve disciples. He's also the author of three letters that are collected later in the Bible—1 John, 2 John, and 3 John—as well as the book of Revelation. The "other" John mentioned in the first chapter of the book of John is John the Baptist. John the Baptist was Jesus's cousin. He baptized Jesus and talked about Jesus to people all over the region right before Jesus began traveling, teaching, and healing people. But really, both Johns are witnesses to Jesus's ministry and model how we can be witnesses for Jesus with our words and deeds.

The Rhythms of Our Lives

SETTING UP THE STORY

The story we're going to read today takes what happened in Genesis 1 and expands on how ancient followers of God—the ancestors of our faith—understood the way God created us. It's considered to be a second version of the creation story. Remember that these early believers were seeking ways of understanding their lives and their relationship to God. This second story is told by God's followers to communicate the importance of that relationship. When we read this chapter of Genesis, listen for what mattered most to the storyteller and to God.

READ: GENESIS 2 (MSG)

Heaven and Earth were finished,
  down to the last detail.
By the seventh day
    God had finished his work.
  On the seventh day
    he rested from all his work.
God blessed the seventh day.
    He made it a Holy Day
Because on that day he rested from his work,
    all the creating God had done.
This is the story of how it all started,
    of Heaven and Earth when they were created.
At the time God made Earth and Heaven, before any grasses or shrubs had sprouted from the ground—God hadn't yet sent rain on Earth, nor was there anyone around to work the ground (the whole Earth was

watered by underground springs)—GOD formed Man out of dirt from the ground and blew into his nostrils the breath of life. The Man came alive—a living soul!

Then GOD planted a garden in Eden, in the east. He put the Man he had just made in it. GOD made all kinds of trees grow from the ground, trees beautiful to look at and good to eat. The Tree-of-Life was in the middle of the garden, also the Tree-of-Knowledge-of-Good-and-Evil.

A river flows out of Eden to water the garden and from there divides into four rivers. The first is named Pishon; it flows through Havilah where there is gold. The gold of this land is good. The land is also known for a sweet-scented resin and the onyx stone. The second river is named Gihon; it flows through the land of Cush. The third river is named Hiddekel and flows east of Assyria. The fourth river is the Euphrates.

GOD took the Man and set him down in the Garden of Eden to work the ground and keep it in order.

GOD commanded the Man, "You can eat from any tree in the garden, except from the Tree-of-Knowledge-of-Good-and-Evil. Don't eat from it. The moment you eat from that tree, you're dead."

GOD said, "It's not good for the Man to be alone; I'll make him a helper, a companion." So GOD formed from the dirt of the ground all the animals of the field and all the birds of the air. He brought them to the Man to see what he would name them. Whatever the Man called each living creature, that was its name. The Man named the cattle, named the birds of the air, named the wild animals; but he didn't find a suitable companion.

GOD put the Man into a deep sleep. As he slept he removed one of his ribs and replaced it with flesh. GOD then used the rib that he had taken from the Man to make Woman and presented her to the Man.

The Man said,
"Finally! Bone of my bone,
    flesh of my flesh!
Name her Woman
    for she was made from Man."

Therefore a man leaves his father and mother and embraces his wife. They become one flesh.

The two of them, the Man and his Wife, were naked, but they felt no shame.

TALK ABOUT IT

- What are a few things God says are important in this chapter?
- In all of creation, what's the first thing God says is "not good"?
- Why do you think God gives Adam the job of naming all of the animals?
- What jobs do you have?
- If you were going to create the world, what would you do differently?
- Why do you think God chose to create things the way he did?
- Is there anything that confuses you about this story? If so, it's okay! Do you have any questions about Genesis 2? It's time to ask your questions about the Bible.

CLOSING THOUGHT

Relationship—with each other, with God, and with creation—is the major note in today's story. God says that it isn't good for man to be alone, so he makes a companion for him. They are so close that Adam calls Eve "bone of my bones, flesh of my flesh," and they don't even feel embarrassed about being naked! (I'm sure you didn't miss that part of the story!)

God also gives humans the responsibility of taking care of the world he created and taking care of each other in that world. We don't all have to be farmers in order to take care of the world. And we don't all have to be doctors in order to take care of other people. We each have different gifts that help us build healthy relationships with people and God, and that helps us take care of the world.

PRAYER PROMPT

Today, let's be thankful for our relationships with our family, our friends, our pets, and our God! Who are you thankful for? Let's each take a turn praying for the people in our lives we're grateful for and ask God for help showing our love to one another through the gifts he has given us.

ACTIVITY: FORM FROM PLAY-DOH

The Genesis 2 story describes God forming Adam from the dust and then breathing life into him. We learned in Genesis 1 that we are made in God's image. Humans are makers too. We love to build and design and draw and create. The ways we can be creative together are limitless. Choose your favorite medium for art (or even Play-Doh!) and create something that reminds you of a person you love. It could even be a gift to that person.

Water of Life

The story of Genesis 2 mentions one river that divides into four separate headwaters. Just like today, water is a source and metaphor for life. The river flows from Eden all throughout the region in which the people lived, bringing fruit and growth and life. When Jesus walked the Earth, he often used water as a symbol for life, calling himself the source of Living Water, and declaring that whoever believes in him will have rivers of living water flowing from within them (John 7:38). Through Jesus Christ and the power of the Holy Spirit, we can be like the Garden of Eden, fruitful and vibrant and filled with life, every day.

When We Lost the Rhythm

SETTING UP THE STORY

In the first creation story, we learned that God created the heavens and the earth. Everything is declared good, including that humankind is made in the image and likeness of God. In the second creation story, we learn *why* God created the heavens and the earth—for relationship. Today's chapter of Genesis is a continuation of the second creation story. Let's see what happens to Adam and Eve in this chapter of the story.

READ: GENESIS 3 (NLT)

The serpent was the shrewdest of all the wild animals the LORD God had made. One day he asked the woman, "Did God really say you must not eat the fruit from any of the trees in the garden?"

"Of course we may eat fruit from the trees in the garden," the woman replied. "It's only the fruit from the tree in the middle of the garden that we are not allowed to eat. God said, 'You must not eat it or even touch it; if you do, you will die.'"

"You won't die!" the serpent replied to the woman. "God knows that your eyes will be opened as soon as you eat it, and you will be like God, knowing both good and evil."

The woman was convinced. She saw that the tree was beautiful and its fruit looked delicious, and she wanted the wisdom it would give her. So she took some of the fruit and ate it. Then she gave some to her husband, who was with her, and he ate it, too. At that moment their eyes were opened, and they suddenly felt shame at their nakedness. So they sewed fig leaves together to cover themselves.

When the cool evening breezes were blowing, the man and his wife heard the LORD God walking about in the garden. So they hid from the L ORD God among the trees. Then the L ORD God called to the man, "Where are you?"

He replied, "I heard you walking in the garden, so I hid. I was afraid because I was naked."

"Who told you that you were naked?" the L ORD God asked. "Have you eaten from the tree whose fruit I commanded you not to eat?"

The man replied, "It was the woman you gave me who gave me the fruit, and I ate it."

Then the L ORD God asked the woman, "What have you done?"

"The serpent deceived me," she replied. "That's why I ate it."

Then the L ORD God said to the serpent,

"Because you have done this, you are cursed
    more than all animals, domestic and wild.
You will crawl on your belly,
    groveling in the dust as long as you live.
And I will cause hostility between you and the woman,
    and between your offspring and her offspring.
He will strike your head,
    and you will strike his heel."

Then he said to the woman,

"I will sharpen the pain of your pregnancy,
    and in pain you will give birth.
And you will desire to control your husband,
    but he will rule over you."

And to the man he said,

"Since you listened to your wife and ate from the tree
    whose fruit I commanded you not to eat,
the ground is cursed because of you.
    All your life you will struggle to scratch a living from it.
It will grow thorns and thistles for you,
    though you will eat of its grains.
By the sweat of your brow
    will you have food to eat
until you return to the ground

from which you were made.
  For you were made from dust,
    and to dust you will return."

Then the man—Adam—named his wife Eve, because she would be the mother of all who live. And the LORD God made clothing from animal skins for Adam and his wife.

Then the LORD God said, "Look, the human beings have become like us, knowing both good and evil. What if they reach out, take fruit from the tree of life, and eat it? Then they will live forever!" So the LORD God banished them from the Garden of Eden, and he sent Adam out to cultivate the ground from which he had been made. After sending them out, the LORD God stationed mighty cherubim to the east of the Garden of Eden. And he placed a flaming sword that flashed back and forth to guard the way to the tree of life.

TALK ABOUT IT

- Have you ever been told you couldn't eat something that looked really good? How did that make you feel?
- Are you ever tempted to eat the thing you've been told you can't?
- Have you ever given in to temptation? Did you get in trouble when someone found out?
- Whose fault was it that Adam and Eve ate the fruit from the tree in the middle of the garden (the Tree of Knowledge of Good and Evil)?
- What do you think about the talking serpent?
- Is there anything that confuses you about this story? If so, it's okay! Do you have any questions about Genesis 3? It's time to ask your questions about the Bible.

CLOSING THOUGHT

Last time we learned how important relationship is to God. When we are in good, healthy relationships, the love we have for each other breaks down our barriers. Our relationships are like a beautiful dance together.

Today's story shows what happens when we are out of step with God. One way to think about sin is to think about being out of step with the way things ought to be. Adam and Eve chose to eat the fruit of the one tree God had said they shouldn't eat from—the Tree of Knowledge of Good and Evil. The consequences of their sin not only hurt themselves, but all the other people that followed them.

Removing Adam and Eve from the Garden of Eden may seem like a harsh punishment, but it actually reveals God's mercy and love. He did not want them to eat from that tree and live forever in their sin. God had a plan to save them (and all people) from sin.

PRAYER PROMPT

Because God cares so much about a relationship with us, he loves to listen to us and to be with us. We can tell God anything when we pray to him. This is called confession. Confession is sometimes more difficult than just thanking God for all we have. In our prayer time today, let's each name one way we've gotten out of step with someone and ask God to give us his strength to love one another better.

ACTIVITY: DANCE PARTY

All this talk about rhythm makes me want to jump up and dance! Turn on your favorite tunes and groove with your family this week. Let loose, have fun, be silly, and party like you're back in the Garden of Eden, carefree and unselfconscious. Watch out for other people's toes, though!

How Many "Kinds" Did God Create?

When Adam and Eve left the Garden of Eden, they entered a big world. Our understanding of how big that world is just keeps growing! Scientists estimate that our planet holds around 8.7 million different species of living things, give or take 1.3 million. About one quarter of all those species live in the ocean. And we're still discovering more!

The Great Divide

SETTING UP THE STORY

The Bible is filled with stories of people who do great things for one another, and it also tells about people who do awful things to one another. Some of the stories we're going to read seem downright brutal. When we let our own self-interests drive our decisions without regard for others, people get hurt. It happens between brothers and sisters, parents and children, friends at school, neighbors in communities, and people who hold different viewpoints, all around the world. Today's story shows us what happens when we look to our own self-interests instead of practicing love.

READ: GENESIS 4:1–18 (MSG)

Adam slept with Eve his wife. She conceived and had Cain. She said, "I've gotten a man, with GOD's help!"

Then she had another baby, Abel. Abel was a herdsman and Cain a farmer.

Time passed. Cain brought an offering to GOD from the produce of his farm. Abel also brought an offering, but from the firstborn animals of his herd, choice cuts of meat. GOD liked Abel and his offering, but Cain and his offering didn't get his approval. Cain lost his temper and went into a sulk.

GOD spoke to Cain: "Why this tantrum? Why the sulking? If you do well, won't you be accepted? And if you don't do well, sin is lying in wait for you, ready to pounce; it's out to get you, you've got to master it."

Cain had words with his brother. They were out in the field; Cain came at Abel his brother and killed him.

GOD said to Cain, "Where is Abel your brother?"

He said, "How should I know? Am I his babysitter?"

God said, "What have you done! The voice of your brother's blood is calling to me from the ground. From now on you'll get nothing but curses from this ground; you'll be driven from this ground that has opened its arms to receive the blood of your murdered brother. You'll farm this ground, but it will no longer give you its best. You'll be a homeless wanderer on Earth."

Cain said to God, "My punishment is too much. I can't take it! You've thrown me off the land and I can never again face you. I'm a homeless wanderer on Earth and whoever finds me will kill me."

God told him, "No. Anyone who kills Cain will pay for it seven times over." God put a mark on Cain to protect him so that no one who met him would kill him.

Cain left the presence of God and lived in No-Man's-Land, east of Eden.

Cain slept with his wife. She conceived and had Enoch. He then built a city and named it after his son, Enoch.

Enoch had Irad,

Irad had Mehujael,

Mehujael had Methushael,

Methushael had Lamech.

TALK ABOUT IT
- Why did Cain kill his brother, Abel?
- What emotions did Cain feel in today's story?
- How does God advise Cain to deal with his anger?
- What is Cain's punishment for killing Abel?
- Is there anything that confuses you about this story? If so, it's okay! Do you have any questions about Genesis 4:1–18? It's time to ask your questions about the Bible.

CLOSING THOUGHT

The difference between Cain and Abel didn't have much to do with what offering they brought. God was more concerned with their hearts. Cain brought some of his veggies (not the "first fruits"), and Abel brought his best to God ("some of the firstborn," which had the best meat). Abel's heart was focused on *giving his best* to God. But Cain's heart was focused on *being the best* before God. Then Cain acted out of jealousy and anger, committed murder, and became separated from his family and God.

Sin causes us to focus on ourselves, but God desires people to focus on him and to walk in his ways.

PRAYER PROMPT

We hear all day long about love, but what does love look like? One of the most famous passages in the Bible says, "Love is patient, love is kind." Even though God punished Cain for his sin, God also protected him. He was patient and kind. As we pray together, let's think about ways we can be more patient with and kind to each other.

ACTIVITY: "LOVE IS PATIENT AND KIND" COLLAGE

Look up 1 Corinthians 13 and use the words that stand out to you to make a collage of things that remind you of God's love.

What's the Deal with the Lists of Names?

At the end of our passage today is the beginning of a list of children and grandchildren, descendants of Cain, that might make your head spin a little. There is purpose behind every story we find in the Bible, and these long lists of names aren't any different. Lists of names were included in the Bible to establish the nation's identity and roots. The list of names and the stories associated with those names shaped the people's understanding of their position in the world.

Those People

SETTING UP THE STORY

Last time we read about how sin divides us and the harm we can do to each other out of jealousy, envy, and hatred. In the story of Cain and Abel, the thing that caused separation was the way the two men worshipped God. Divisions between people over their differences continued into Jesus's time and are still happening today. Let's see how Jesus handled division during his time.

READ: JOHN 4:1–42 (NIV)

Now Jesus learned that the Pharisees had heard that he was gaining and baptizing more disciples than John—although in fact it was not Jesus who baptized, but his disciples. So he left Judea and went back once more to Galilee.

Now he had to go through Samaria. So he came to a town in Samaria called Sychar, near the plot of ground Jacob had given to his son Joseph. Jacob's well was there, and Jesus, tired as he was from the journey, sat down by the well. It was about noon.

When a Samaritan woman came to draw water, Jesus said to her, "Will you give me a drink?" (His disciples had gone into the town to buy food.)

The Samaritan woman said to him, "You are a Jew and I am a Samaritan woman. How can you ask me for a drink?" (For Jews do not associate with Samaritans.)

Jesus answered her, "If you knew the gift of God and who it is that asks you for a drink, you would have asked him and he would have given you living water."

"Sir," the woman said, "you have nothing to draw with and the well is deep. Where can you get this living water? Are you greater than our father

Jacob, who gave us the well and drank from it himself, as did also his sons and his livestock?"

Jesus answered, "Everyone who drinks this water will be thirsty again, but whoever drinks the water I give them will never thirst. Indeed, the water I give them will become in them a spring of water welling up to eternal life."

The woman said to him, "Sir, give me this water so that I won't get thirsty and have to keep coming here to draw water."

He told her, "Go, call your husband and come back."

"I have no husband," she replied.

Jesus said to her, "You are right when you say you have no husband. The fact is, you have had five husbands, and the man you now have is not your husband. What you have just said is quite true."

"Sir," the woman said, "I can see that you are a prophet. Our ancestors worshiped on this mountain, but you Jews claim that the place where we must worship is in Jerusalem."

"Woman," Jesus replied, "believe me, a time is coming when you will worship the Father neither on this mountain nor in Jerusalem. You Samaritans worship what you do not know; we worship what we do know, for salvation is from the Jews. Yet a time is coming and has now come when the true worshipers will worship the Father in the Spirit and in truth, for they are the kind of worshipers the Father seeks. God is spirit, and his worshipers must worship in the Spirit and in truth."

The woman said, "I know that Messiah" (called Christ) "is coming. When he comes, he will explain everything to us."

Then Jesus declared, "I, the one speaking to you—I am he."

Just then his disciples returned and were surprised to find him talking with a woman. But no one asked, "What do you want?" or "Why are you talking with her?"

Then, leaving her water jar, the woman went back to the town and said to the people, "Come, see a man who told me everything I ever did. Could this be the Messiah?" They came out of the town and made their way toward him.

Meanwhile his disciples urged him, "Rabbi, eat something."

But he said to them, "I have food to eat that you know nothing about."

Then his disciples said to each other, "Could someone have brought him food?"

"My food," said Jesus, "is to do the will of him who sent me and to finish his work. Don't you have a saying, 'It's still four months until harvest'? I tell you, open your eyes and look at the fields! They are ripe for harvest. Even now the one who reaps draws a wage and harvests a crop for eternal life, so that the sower and the reaper may be glad together. Thus the saying 'One sows and another reaps' is true. I sent you to reap what you have not worked for. Others have done the hard work, and you have reaped the benefits of their labor."

Many of the Samaritans from that town believed in him because of the woman's testimony, "He told me everything I ever did." So when the Samaritans came to him, they urged him to stay with them, and he stayed two days. And because of his words many more became believers.

They said to the woman, "We no longer believe just because of what you said; now we have heard for ourselves, and we know that this man really is the Savior of the world."

TALK ABOUT IT
- What does Jesus call himself in this story?
- Who helps other people meet Jesus in today's story?
- Why were the disciples surprised that Jesus was talking to the Samaritan woman?
- Are there people in your life that you avoid because they are different? What makes them different?
- Is there anything that confuses you about this story? If so, it's okay! Do you have any questions about John 4:1–42? It's time to ask your questions about the Bible.

CLOSING THOUGHT
In Jesus's time, just like today, some groups of people avoided other groups of people. The Samaritans did not hang out with the Jews, and they

certainly didn't ask them to eat or drink together. What's more, men in Jesus's day didn't teach or even talk with women who were not related to them. And yet here we see Jesus sitting by a well with a Samaritans women, sharing for the first time that he is the Messiah, the Son of God!

Jesus is constantly turning our ideas upside down, breaking the barriers between people to build bridges of peace, love, and unity. Jesus says that even those who have been called unworthy (Samaritans, women) are worthy of love, salvation, and grace.

PRAYER PROMPT

Do you know anyone who is treated badly because he or she is different? Maybe this person has skin of another color, or maybe they are from another country, or speak another language. Let's ask God to help us see people through his eyes, as fellow children of God, who deserve the same love, mercy, and kindness that God has shown us. Pray that God will help us love differences rather than be separated by them as the Jews and Samaritans were.

ACTIVITY: MEET AT THE WELL

If you live in an area that has homeless, consider preparing a care kit for them. There are some great ideas for how to approach someone who is homeless and what to pack in your care kit online.[1] Another option is to identify a local organization that is serving those in the community who are refugees or recent immigrants to find out what needs they have and how you can help.

Who Were the Samaritans?

The Samaritans and Jews were two sets of people with similar roots but different beliefs. Because of their differences, they did *not* get along. Their biggest fight was over where people were supposed to worship God. The Jews believed it was Mount Zion, and the Samaritans believed it was Mount Gerizim. In today's story, Jesus aimed to put an end to the whole dispute by revealing what God really cares about—not *where* we worship (on a specific mountain), but *how* to worship him (in spirit and in truth).

Noah's Ark

SETTING UP THE STORY

Like creation stories, early tribes of people all over the world have different versions of the flood story we have in our Bible. Just as we seek to understand what happens in our world and in our lives, the early followers of God tried to understand the terrible things humans have done and the natural disasters that shaped, destroyed, and rebuilt their worlds.

READ: EXCERPTS BELOW FROM GENESIS 6–8 (MSG)

The full story of Noah is three chapters long, beginning with Genesis 6:9 through 8:22. Here is an alternate reading option to help keep the attention of children. You should decide for yourselves if you want to read the full version together and look it up in your own preferred translation.

This is the story of Noah: Noah was a good man, a man of integrity in his community. Noah walked with God. Noah had three sons: Shem, Ham, and Japheth.

As far as God was concerned, the Earth had become a sewer; there was violence everywhere. God took one look and saw how bad it was, everyone corrupt and corrupting—life itself corrupt to the core.

God said to Noah, "It's all over. It's the end of the human race. The violence is everywhere; I'm making a clean sweep.

"Build yourself a ship from teakwood. Make rooms in it. Coat it with pitch inside and out. Make it 450 feet long, seventy-five feet wide, and forty-five feet high. Build a roof for it and put in a window eighteen inches from the top; put in a door on the side of the ship; and make three decks, lower, middle, and upper.

"I'm going to bring a flood on the Earth that will destroy everything alive under Heaven. Total destruction.

"But I'm going to establish a covenant with you: You'll board the ship, and your sons, your wife and your sons' wives will come on board with you. You are also to take two of each living creature, a male and a female, on board the ship, to preserve their lives with you: two of every species of bird, mammal, and reptile—two of everything so as to preserve their lives along with yours. Also get all the food you'll need and store it up for you and them."

Noah did everything God commanded him to do. (Genesis 6:9–22)

Next GOD said to Noah, "Now board the ship, you and all your family—out of everyone in this generation, you're the righteous one.

"Take on board with you seven pairs of every clean animal, a male and a female; one pair of every unclean animal, a male and a female; and seven pairs of every kind of bird, a male and a female, to insure their survival on Earth. In just seven days I will dump rain on Earth for forty days and forty nights. I'll make a clean sweep of everything that I've made."

Noah did everything GOD commanded him. (7:1–5)

It was the six-hundredth year of Noah's life, in the second month, on the seventeenth day of the month that it happened: all the underground springs erupted and all the windows of Heaven were thrown open. Rain poured for forty days and forty nights. (7:11–12)

The flood continued forty days and the waters rose and lifted the ship high over the Earth. The waters kept rising, the flood deepened on the Earth, the ship floated on the surface. The flood got worse until all the highest mountains were covered—the high-water mark reached twenty feet above the crest of the mountains. Everything died. Anything that moved—dead. Birds, farm animals, wild animals, the entire teeming exuberance of life—dead. And all people—dead. Every living, breathing creature that lived on dry land died; he wiped out the whole works—people and animals, crawling creatures and flying birds, every last one of them, gone. Only Noah and his company on the ship lived. (7:17–23)

Then God turned his attention to Noah and all the wild animals and farm animals with him on the ship. God caused the wind to blow and the floodwaters began to go down. The underground springs were shut off, the windows of Heaven closed and the rain quit. Inch by inch the water lowered. After 150 days the worst was over. (8:1–3)

After forty days Noah opened the window that he had built into the ship.

He sent out a raven; it flew back and forth waiting for the floodwaters to dry up. Then he sent a dove to check on the flood conditions, but it couldn't even find a place to perch—water still covered the Earth. Noah reached out and caught it, brought it back into the ship.

He waited seven more days and sent out the dove again. It came back in the evening with a freshly picked olive leaf in its beak. Noah knew that the flood was about finished.

He waited another seven days and sent the dove out a third time. This time it didn't come back.

In the six-hundred-first year of Noah's life, on the first day of the first month, the flood had dried up. Noah opened the hatch of the ship and saw dry ground. By the twenty-seventh day of the second month, the Earth was completely dry.

God spoke to Noah: "Leave the ship, you and your wife and your sons and your sons' wives. And take all the animals with you, the whole menagerie of birds and mammals and crawling creatures, all that brimming prodigality of life, so they can reproduce and flourish on the Earth."

Noah disembarked with his sons and wife and his sons' wives. Then all the animals, crawling creatures, birds—every creature on the face of the Earth—left the ship family by family.

Noah built an altar to God. He selected clean animals and birds from every species and offered them as burnt offerings on the altar. God smelled the sweet fragrance and thought to himself, "I'll never again curse the ground because of people. I know they have this bent toward evil from an early age, but I'll never again kill off everything living as I've just done.

For as long as Earth lasts,
    planting and harvest, cold and heat,
   Summer and winter, day and night
    will never stop." (8:6–22)

TALK ABOUT IT

- Why did God send the flood?
- With all the awful things that happen in the world, do you ever feel like it'd be better to just start over?
- What are some natural disasters in our day?
- When natural disasters occur in our world, what are some of the ways we comfort each other?
- Is there anything that confuses you about this story? If so, it's okay! Do you have any questions about the story of Noah? It's time to ask your questions about the Bible.

CLOSING THOUGHT

Imagine not having access to twenty-four-hour news and weather stations that alert you to storm warnings and predict what's to come so that you know how to prepare. In the story of Noah, God is like the weatherman, telling Noah what he should expect so he can be prepared.

Just as we do today, the early followers of God were trying to figure out the meaning of life and why things happen. The story of Noah teaches us a part of the truth about our God. Our God is a protector. He is a shelter in the storm. He is ever-present, even in times we feel most alone and frightened. He makes promises to the people he created, and he is faithful to his promises.

PRAYER PROMPT

What is happening in your family's life right now that seems dark and scary? What is happening in the world right now that seems frightening? Confess together these things, and then pray together Psalm 121 (MSG):

> I look up to the mountains;
>   does my strength come from mountains?
> No, my strength comes from GOD,
>   who made heaven, and earth, and mountains.
> He won't let you stumble,
>   your Guardian God won't fall asleep.

Not on your life! Israel's
   Guardian will never doze or sleep.
GOD's your Guardian,
   right at your side to protect you—
Shielding you from sunstroke,
   sheltering you from moonstroke.
GOD guards you from every evil,
   he guards your very life.
He guards you when you leave and when you return,
   he guards you now, he guards you always.

ACTIVITY: LIVING ROOM ARK

Pretend your family is Noah's, and the flood's coming! Can you make yourself an ark? Be creative—push furniture together, gather up stuffed animals, and ride as a family through the (pretend) waves, holding on to one another in God's love and protection.

Ham, Shem, Japheth

Noah's three sons named in the Bible are Ham, Shem, and Japheth—three names given to specific ethnic groups. Ham, Shem, and Japheth are said to be the fathers of the Hamites, Semites, and Japhetites. The early followers of God believed that the world was divided into these three ethnic groups as arranged by the known continents at the time—Europe, Asia, and Africa.

The Story of the Lost Son

SETTING UP THE STORY

Last time we read about Noah and the flood and how God's people tried to understand natural disasters in light of what they understood about God. The people of God who told the story of Noah thought God might be the kind of god that would get fed up with his people and save only the few who were considered "good." The story we'll read today is about a different kind of Father, and it is told by Jesus to help us understand the kind of love our God has for us—*all* of us.

READ: LUKE 15:11–32 (NLT)

Jesus told them this story: "A man had two sons. The younger son told his father, 'I want my share of your estate now before you die.' So his father agreed to divide his wealth between his sons.

"A few days later this younger son packed all his belongings and moved to a distant land, and there he wasted all his money in wild living. About the time his money ran out, a great famine swept over the land, and he began to starve. He persuaded a local farmer to hire him, and the man sent him into his fields to feed the pigs. The young man became so hungry that even the pods he was feeding the pigs looked good to him. But no one gave him anything.

"When he finally came to his senses, he said to himself, 'At home even the hired servants have food enough to spare, and here I am dying of hunger! I will go home to my father and say, "Father, I have sinned against both heaven and you, and I am no longer worthy of being called your son. Please take me on as a hired servant."'

"So he returned home to his father. And while he was still a long way off, his father saw him coming. Filled with love and compassion, he ran to his son, embraced him, and kissed him. His son said to him, 'Father, I have sinned against both heaven and you, and I am no longer worthy of being called your son.'

"But his father said to the servants, 'Quick! Bring the finest robe in the house and put it on him. Get a ring for his finger and sandals for his feet. And kill the calf we have been fattening. We must celebrate with a feast, for this son of mine was dead and has now returned to life. He was lost, but now he is found.' So the party began.

"Meanwhile, the older son was in the fields working. When he returned home, he heard music and dancing in the house, and he asked one of the servants what was going on. 'Your brother is back,' he was told, 'and your father has killed the fattened calf. We are celebrating because of his safe return.'

"The older brother was angry and wouldn't go in. His father came out and begged him, but he replied, 'All these years I've slaved for you and never once refused to do a single thing you told me to. And in all that time you never gave me even one young goat for a feast with my friends. Yet when this son of yours comes back after squandering your money on prostitutes, you celebrate by killing the fattened calf!'

"His father said to him, 'Look, dear son, you have always stayed by me, and everything I have is yours. We had to celebrate this happy day. For your brother was dead and has come back to life! He was lost, but now he is found!'"

TALK ABOUT IT
- How does the father respond to his younger son when the son asks for his inheritance?
- What is the father's response when he sees his younger son coming home?
- How does the older son react to the party given in his brother's honor?
- Do you relate more to the older son or to the younger son? Why?
- Which son does the father love more?

• Is there anything that confuses you about this story? If so, it's okay! Do you have any questions about Luke 15:11–32? It's time to ask your questions about the Bible.

CLOSING THOUGHT

At first it seems as though the younger son is the foolish one and the older son is the good one, but both sons miss the mark. The younger son makes poor choices and then tries to figure out how to get back into his father's favor, and the older son feels entitled and jealous of the father's love and celebration. What the Father wants is for both sons to return to him. He wants both sons to love him and to love one another.

Jesus told this story so people could understand God better. God is the Father in this story. The Father's love is so big that he has no trouble welcoming back the son who made lots of poor choices. The Father's love is so big that he doesn't hesitate to find the son who feels like his good behavior should have earned him greater favor. The Father's love fills every heart and shouts, "You are worthy, you are worthy, you are worthy!"

PRAYER PROMPT

Pray together Psalm 139 (NLT) below, a poem about how intimately God knows us, how present he is with us, and how committed he is to guiding us through his Holy Spirit to a life filled with faith, hope, and joy. (The psalms are poems or songs written to God. They are an example of the range of emotions and thoughts we can bring to God, even those things we wouldn't confess to anyone else!)

O Lord, you have examined my heart
    and know everything about me.
You know when I sit down or stand up.
    You know my thoughts even when I'm far away.
You see me when I travel
    and when I rest at home.

You know everything I do.
You know what I am going to say
    even before I say it, LORD.
You go before me and follow me.
    You place your hand of blessing on my head.
Such knowledge is too wonderful for me,
    too great for me to understand!

I can never escape from your Spirit!
    I can never get away from your presence!
If I go up to heaven, you are there;
    if I go down to the grave, you are there.
If I ride the wings of the morning,
    if I dwell by the farthest oceans,
even there your hand will guide me,
    and your strength will support me.
I could ask the darkness to hide me
    and the light around me to become night—
        but even in darkness I cannot hide from you.
To you the night shines as bright as day.
    Darkness and light are the same to you.

You made all the delicate, inner parts of my body
    and knit me together in my mother's womb.
Thank you for making me so wonderfully complex!
    Your workmanship is marvelous—how well I know it.
You watched me as I was being formed in utter seclusion,
    as I was woven together in the dark of the womb.
You saw me before I was born.
    Every day of my life was recorded in your book.
Every moment was laid out
    before a single day had passed.

How precious are your thoughts about me, O God.
They cannot be numbered!
I can't even count them;
they outnumber the grains of sand!
And when I wake up,
you are still with me!

O God, if only you would destroy the wicked!
Get out of my life, you murderers!
They blaspheme you;
your enemies misuse your name.
O LORD, shouldn't I hate those who hate you?
Shouldn't I despise those who oppose you?
Yes, I hate them with total hatred,
for your enemies are my enemies.

Search me, O God, and know my heart;
test me and know my anxious thoughts.
Point out anything in me that offends you,
and lead me along the path of everlasting life.

ACTIVITY #1: HIDE AND SEEK

As we read in today's story and prayed through Psalm 139, God seeks us out no matter where we are. So run and hide, kiddos! See how long it takes for your mom or dad to find you.

ACTIVITY #2: FEAST!

Choose a night this week to celebrate how big God's love is and how much he wants us to keep returning to him. Plan a meal of your favorite foods. Prepare the feast together, and when you're ready to dine, give a toast to celebrate something special about each person around the table.

Insincere Apologies

"Father, I have sinned against both heaven and you. I am no longer worthy of being called your son" (Luke 15:21 NLT). The confession that the younger son prepares for his father in today's story would have seemed familiar to the disciples at that time. That sentence sounds a lot like words of confession from Pharaoh in the Exodus story (we'll read more about that later): "I have sinned against the LORD your God and against you" (10:16 NLT). In that story, Pharaoh isn't being sincere but just looking for relief, like the younger son in our story today.

A Future to Hope For

SETTING UP THE STORY

In today's reading, we swing back into the Old Testament to meet the great father of the Jewish faith: Abraham. In this story he's still called Abram. (God gives him a new name later.) When we meet Abram today, God appears to him in a vision and makes some promises that seem kind of hard to believe. We can learn a lot about how we can rely on and relate to God through today's story. Let's jump in!

READ: GENESIS 15 (NIV)

After this, the word of the LORD came to Abram in a vision:

"Do not be afraid, Abram.
  I am your shield,
  your very great reward."

But Abram said, "Sovereign LORD, what can you give me since I remain childless and the one who will inherit my estate is Eliezer of Damascus?" And Abram said, "You have given me no children; so a servant in my household will be my heir."

Then the word of the LORD came to him: "This man will not be your heir, but a son who is your own flesh and blood will be your heir." He took him outside and said, "Look up at the sky and count the stars—if indeed you can count them." Then he said to him, "So shall your offspring be."

Abram believed the LORD, and he credited it to him as righteousness.

He also said to him, "I am the LORD, who brought you out of Ur of the Chaldeans to give you this land to take possession of it."

But Abram said, "Sovereign LORD, how can I know that I will gain possession of it?"

So the LORD said to him, "Bring me a heifer, a goat and a ram, each three years old, along with a dove and a young pigeon."

Abram brought all these to him, cut them in two and arranged the halves opposite each other; the birds, however, he did not cut in half. Then birds of prey came down on the carcasses, but Abram drove them away.

As the sun was setting, Abram fell into a deep sleep, and a thick and dreadful darkness came over him. Then the LORD said to him, "Know for certain that for four hundred years your descendants will be strangers in a country not their own and that they will be enslaved and mistreated there. But I will punish the nation they serve as slaves, and afterward they will come out with great possessions. You, however, will go to your ancestors in peace and be buried at a good old age. In the fourth generation your descendants will come back here, for the sin of the Amorites has not yet reached its full measure."

When the sun had set and darkness had fallen, a smoking firepot with a blazing torch appeared and passed between the pieces. On that day the LORD made a covenant with Abram and said, "To your descendants I give this land, from the Wadi of Egypt to the great river, the Euphrates— the land of the Kenites, Kenizzites, Kadmonites, Hittites, Perizzites, Rephaites, Amorites, Canaanites, Girgashites and Jebusites."

TALK ABOUT IT

- Why do you think God tells Abram not to be afraid?
- How would you describe the conversation between God and Abram?
- What do you learn about how God interacts with people through this story?
- Have you or anyone in your family ever thought something wasn't possible, only for that thing to happen?
- Is there anything that confuses you about this story? If so, it's okay! Do you have any questions about Genesis 15? It's time to ask your questions about the Bible.

CLOSING THOUGHT

God establishes a *covenant* with Abram in today's story. A covenant is an agreement, like a promise, between two groups. It's a bond that creates a relationship. (For example, a marriage is considered a covenant.) When God sets a covenant with his people, it is unconditional. That means there's nothing we can do to shatter that bond or break his commitment to us. It never expires—God's love and commitment to us extends throughout our lives and beyond into eternity.

In the Old Testament, covenants were often tied to the sacrifice of animals, which would have symbolized their worth and significance to the people. Today, when we form a covenant in marriage, the couples usually exchange rings as symbols of the significance of their relationship. Aren't you glad we don't do the animal sacrifice thing anymore?

PRAYER PROMPT

In today's Scripture passage, Abram isn't afraid to question God about what he has promised. Jesus tells his followers in the New Testament, "Ask and it will be given to you; seek and you will find; knock and the door will be opened to you" (Matthew 7:7 NIV). Don't be afraid to ask God to show you the way. If your family has a story of God's faithfulness that you shared today, thank God for his mercies and graces. If not, ask God to reveal moments you might have overlooked and ask him to help you see his work in your daily lives.

ACTIVITY #1: STORY MAP

What did it take for your family to come together where you live today? Map out your family's story! Make a timeline of the major highs and lows that have happened in your life and your family's life.

ACTIVITY #2: THE STARS IN THE SKY

In today's story, God tells Abram what he has to look forward to in the future, and it's more than he can imagine—children?! Descendants to out-number the stars?! Draw or paint a picture of the night sky. Fill it with stars, the moon, even other planets. Leave room on the picture to write the words of God: "Do not be afraid. I am your shield."

Future Now

In Genesis 15, God and Abram have a conversation about what the future is going to look like for his descendants four hundred years down the road. It's both a hard vision and an amazing vision—God tells Abram that things will be tough and his people will suffer under slavery, but one day his descendants will possess the land.

It's also a vision that was written by the people who lived four hundred years or so after Abram, from the people who already had possession of the land. Remember how these stories were written to pass along the stories of faith? This is another chapter that helped to explain the Israelites' journey.

By telling this story, the Israelites staked their claims on the land they possessed by saying God had given that land to them. They were preparing the next generation by telling them where they came from, braiding a sense of purpose into their lives.

Change of Plans

SETTING UP THE STORY

The birth of babies is one of the most mysterious and miraculous events, and it happens every second of every day (four births per second!).[2] Many of the Old Testament stories we'll read talk about how women had a hard time getting pregnant. Our last story talked about how God promised Abram descendants that would outnumber the stars, even though his wife, Sarai, had never been able to conceive. Today, we'll hear about an unexpected pregnancy that changed the entire world.

READ: LUKE 1:26–56 (MSG)

In the sixth month of Elizabeth's pregnancy, God sent the angel Gabriel to the Galilean village of Nazareth to a virgin engaged to be married to a man descended from David. His name was Joseph, and the virgin's name, Mary. Upon entering, Gabriel greeted her:

Good morning!

You're beautiful with God's beauty,

Beautiful inside and out!

God be with you.

She was thoroughly shaken, wondering what was behind a greeting like that. But the angel assured her, "Mary, you have nothing to fear. God has a surprise for you: You will become pregnant and give birth to a son and call his name Jesus.

He will be great,

be called 'Son of the Highest.'

The Lord God will give him

the throne of his father David;

He will rule Jacob's house forever—
> no end, ever, to his kingdom."

Mary said to the angel, "But how? I've never slept with a man."

The angel answered,

The Holy Spirit will come upon you,
> the power of the Highest hover over you;

Therefore, the child you bring to birth
> will be called Holy, Son of God.

"And did you know that your cousin Elizabeth conceived a son, old as she is? Everyone called her barren, and here she is six months pregnant! Nothing, you see, is impossible with God."

And Mary said,

Yes, I see it all now:
> I'm the Lord's maid, ready to serve.

Let it be with me
> just as you say.

Then the angel left her.

Mary didn't waste a minute. She got up and traveled to a town in Judah in the hill country, straight to Zachariah's house, and greeted Elizabeth. When Elizabeth heard Mary's greeting, the baby in her womb leaped. She was filled with the Holy Spirit, and sang out exuberantly,

You're so blessed among women,
> and the babe in your womb, also blessed!

And why am I so blessed that
> the mother of my Lord visits me?

The moment the sound of your
> greeting entered my ears,

The babe in my womb
> skipped like a lamb for sheer joy.

Blessed woman, who believed what God said,
> believed every word would come true!

And Mary said,

I'm bursting with God-news;

I'm dancing the song of my Savior God.
God took one good look at me, and look what happened—
  I'm the most fortunate woman on earth!
What God has done for me will never be forgotten,
  the God whose very name is holy, set apart from all others.
His mercy flows in wave after wave
  on those who are in awe before him.
He bared his arm and showed his strength,
  scattered the bluffing braggarts.
He knocked tyrants off their high horses,
  pulled victims out of the mud.
The starving poor sat down to a banquet;
  the callous rich were left out in the cold.
He embraced his chosen child, Israel;
  he remembered and piled on the mercies, piled them high.
It's exactly what he promised,
  beginning with Abraham and right up to now.
Mary stayed with Elizabeth for three months and then went back to her own home.

TALK ABOUT IT

- How did Mary respond to the angel's news?
- How do you think Mary felt when she met the angel? Close your eyes and try to imagine what that was like. What do you see?
- How do you think Mary felt when she went to visit Elizabeth?
- How do you think the people in Mary's life would have reacted to the news of her pregnancy?
- What do you learn about God in these verses?
- Is there anything that confuses you about this story? If so, it's okay! Do you have any questions about Luke 1:26–56? It's time to ask your questions about the Bible.

CLOSING THOUGHT

This angel's news for Mary was definitely unexpected. She didn't plan on being pregnant before she married Joseph. And Elizabeth hadn't planned on spending most of her life childless.

When Mary first walked into Elizabeth's home, she probably felt worried about how her relative would receive her. Maybe she would condemn her. Maybe she would doubt her story. Maybe she would send her away. Instead, Elizabeth celebrated Mary and called her blessed.

Imagine what it would be like to be greeted by someone the way Elizabeth greeted Mary. You'd be inspired to sing a song of God's great love and mercy too!

PRAYER PROMPT

When unexpected events happen in our lives, we can feel blindsided, afraid, confused, disappointed, angry, surprised, and shocked. God is listening—whether we're feeling thankful or hateful, frustrated or at peace. As you pray together, think about something that happened recently that you didn't expect, and tell God how it made you feel. Then pray that God will help you work through those emotions and will send a friend like Elizabeth to encourage you.

ACTIVITY: BABY SHOWER CARE PACKAGE

Expectant moms today experience a lot of the same worries and fears Mary likely experienced when she first found out she was pregnant. Some new moms don't have family and friends to support them. Contact your local women's shelter or pregnancy support services to find out about their needs, and go on a shopping spree! Shower a new mom in need, and by doing so, you'll be serving Jesus.

Weddings and Families in Biblical Times

Weddings and marriages have changed dramatically since Jesus's time! In Jesus's time, girls were betrothed (or promised) for marriage when they were as young as twelve years old, and boys were betrothed as young as thirteen. The betrothed couple would be considered married, but they wouldn't sleep together right away, sometimes waiting as long as seven years from the time of their legal marriage. When a girl married a boy, the agreement often involved an exchange of property.

The One True God
Who Gives

SETTING UP THE STORY

It's been about forty years since God promised Abram descendants that would outnumber the stars. In that time, Abram had a son named Ishmael, who was born by his wife's servant (this was a common practice in ancient cultures because having an heir was so important). While Ishmael was Abram's firstborn son, he wasn't Sarai's child. This caused all kinds of family trouble (see Genesis 16 and Genesis 21:8–21, if you're up to it). During those years, Abram's name changed from Abram (which means "exalted father") to Abraham (which means "father of many"), and Sarai (which means "quarrelsome") changed to Sarah (which means "princess"). Isaac—the promised son of Abraham and Sarah—was born twenty-five years after the original promise. When we meet Abraham and Isaac today, Isaac is probably around fifteen years old.

READ: GENESIS 22:1–19 (NLT)

Some time later, God tested Abraham's faith. "Abraham!" God called.

"Yes," he replied. "Here I am."

"Take your son, your only son—yes, Isaac, whom you love so much—and go to the land of Moriah. Go and sacrifice him as a burnt offering on one of the mountains, which I will show you."

The next morning Abraham got up early. He saddled his donkey and took two of his servants with him, along with his son, Isaac. Then he chopped wood for a fire for a burnt offering and set out for the place God had told him about. On the third day of their journey, Abraham looked up and saw the place in the distance. "Stay here with the donkey," Abraham told the servants. "The boy and I will travel a little farther. We will worship there, and then we will come right back."

So Abraham placed the wood for the burnt offering on Isaac's shoulders, while he himself carried the fire and the knife. As the two of them walked on together, Isaac turned to Abraham and said, "Father?"

"Yes, my son?" Abraham replied.

"We have the fire and the wood," the boy said, "but where is the sheep for the burnt offering?"

"God will provide a sheep for the burnt offering, my son," Abraham answered. And they both walked on together.

When they arrived at the place where God had told him to go, Abraham built an altar and arranged the wood on it. Then he tied his son, Isaac, and laid him on the altar on top of the wood. And Abraham picked up the knife to kill his son as a sacrifice. At that moment the angel of the Lord called to him from heaven, "Abraham! Abraham!"

"Yes," Abraham replied. "Here I am!"

"Don't lay a hand on the boy!" the angel said. "Do not hurt him in any way, for now I know that you truly fear God. You have not withheld from me even your son, your only son."

Then Abraham looked up and saw a ram caught by its horns in a thicket. So he took the ram and sacrificed it as a burnt offering in place of his son. Abraham named the place Yahweh-Yireh (which means "the Lord will provide"). To this day, people still use that name as a proverb: "On the mountain of the Lord it will be provided."

Then the angel of the Lord called again to Abraham from heaven. "This is what the Lord says: Because you have obeyed me and have not withheld even your son, your only son, I swear by my own name that I will certainly bless you. I will multiply your descendants beyond number, like the stars in the sky and the sand on the seashore. Your descendants will conquer the cities of their enemies. And through your descendants all the nations of the earth will be blessed—all because you have obeyed me."

Then they returned to the servants and traveled back to Beersheba, where Abraham continued to live.

TALK ABOUT IT:

- How do you think Abraham felt when God asked him to sacrifice his son Isaac?
- Are you ever asked by others to do things you don't want to do?
- Put yourself in Isaac's shoes. How would you react to being asked to go through with something so drastic?
- What happens before Abraham has done the unthinkable?
- Is there anything that confuses you about this story? If so, it's okay! Do you have any questions about Genesis 22:1–19? It's time to ask your questions about the Bible.

CLOSING THOUGHT

Just like the Noah story, cultures surrounding Abraham had different ideas about who God was and what God expected from people. As shocking as it may seem, there were many ancient cultures that practiced the ritual of human sacrifice. When God tested Abraham and asked him to sacrifice his beloved son, Isaac, he did so to correct what Abraham had believed about God up to this point. He did so to show how he is different from the false gods of his neighbors.

Our God still doesn't demand the sacrifice of another in order to prove our loyalty. He makes another way, a way of love. A way of peace. A way of mercy. A way of grace. Over and over in the Bible, God corrects and adjusts people's understanding of him. He tells us that he desires mercy, not sacrifice (Hosea 6:6). All that is required of us is to act justly and to love mercy and to walk humbly with God (Micah 6:8).

PRAYER PROMPT

Take turns reading Psalm 40 (NLT) as a prayer today:

I waited patiently for the LORD to help me,
    and he turned to me and heard my cry.
He lifted me out of the pit of despair,
    out of the mud and the mire.
He set my feet on solid ground

and steadied me as I walked along.
He has given me a new song to sing,
  a hymn of praise to our God.
Many will see what he has done and be amazed.
  They will put their trust in the LORD.

Oh, the joys of those who trust the LORD,
  who have no confidence in the proud
  or in those who worship idols.
O LORD my God, you have performed many wonders for us.
  Your plans for us are too numerous to list.
  You have no equal.
If I tried to recite all your wonderful deeds,
  I would never come to the end of them.

You take no delight in sacrifices or offerings.
  Now that you have made me listen, I finally understand—
  you don't require burnt offerings or sin offerings.
Then I said, "Look, I have come.
  As is written about me in the Scriptures:
I take joy in doing your will, my God,
  for your instructions are written on my heart."

I have told all your people about your justice.
  I have not been afraid to speak out,
  as you, O LORD, well know.
I have not kept the good news of your justice hidden in my heart;
  I have talked about your faithfulness and saving power.
I have told everyone in the great assembly
  of your unfailing love and faithfulness.

LORD, don't hold back your tender mercies from me.
  Let your unfailing love and faithfulness always protect me.
For troubles surround me—

too many to count!
My sins pile up so high
   I can't see my way out.
They outnumber the hairs on my head.
   I have lost all courage.

Please, LORD, rescue me!
   Come quickly, LORD, and help me.
May those who try to destroy me
   be humiliated and put to shame.
May those who take delight in my trouble
   be turned back in disgrace.
Let them be horrified by their shame,
   for they said, "Aha! We've got him now!"

But may all who search for you
   be filled with joy and gladness in you.
May those who love your salvation
   repeatedly shout, "The LORD is great!"
As for me, since I am poor and needy,
   let the LORD keep me in his thoughts.
You are my helper and my savior.
   O my God, do not delay.

ACTIVITY: ACT JUSTLY, LOVE MERCY, WALK HUMBLY

What does it mean to do these things? Make a list of words and deeds that you feel define what it means for you to act justly, love mercy, and walk humbly. Hang the list in your bedroom and choose one word to practice this week.

What's in a Name? A Lot! Elohim Versus Jehovah

The Hebrew language is the language that the Old Testament was written in. In Hebrew, there are many different names used for God that mean different things. For example, there are different names meaning "the God who saves," "the God who sees," "God Almighty," etc. In the beginning of Genesis 22, the word used for God is *Elohim*. *Elohim* is a plural form of God and is used to reference God over 2,600 times in the Bible. [3] It's one of the most common names for God in the Bible and means "great strength or power."

But the name given to God when he stops Abraham from sacrificing his son is *Jehovah*. [4] *Jehovah* is the proper name for the Israelite's One True God and is translated for us most often as an all-caps LORD. It is used in the Bible over 6,500 times!

Jesus on the Cross

SETTING UP THE STORY

Last time we learned how God keeps showing his people a better way, proving his love to the people he created. God is always doing things we don't expect him to do. When Jesus came to earth, the people expected him to behave a certain way. They expected him to rule the earth, not to die on a cross. Today's verses show just how little the people understood what Jesus was all about. He's about to be crucified for his strange teachings that contradicted what the religious leaders at the time believed.

READ: MATTHEW 27:32–54 (NIV)

As they were going out, they met a man from Cyrene, named Simon, and they forced him to carry the cross. They came to a place called Golgotha (which means "the place of the skull"). There they offered Jesus wine to drink, mixed with gall; but after tasting it, he refused to drink it. When they had crucified him, they divided up his clothes by casting lots. And sitting down, they kept watch over him there. Above his head they placed the written charge against him: THIS IS JESUS, THE KING OF THE JEWS.

Two rebels were crucified with him, one on his right and one on his left. Those who passed by hurled insults at him, shaking their heads and saying, "You who are going to destroy the temple and build it in three days, save yourself! Come down from the cross, if you are the Son of God!" In the same way the chief priests, the teachers of the law and the elders mocked him. "He saved others," they said, "but he can't save himself! He's the king of Israel! Let him come down now from the cross, and we will believe in him. He trusts in God. Let God rescue him now if he wants him, for he said, 'I am the Son of God.'" In the same way the rebels who were crucified with him also heaped insults on him.

From noon until three in the afternoon darkness came over all the land. About three in the afternoon Jesus cried out in a loud voice, *"Eli, Eli, lema sabachthani?"* (which means "My God, my God, why have you forsaken me?").

When some of those standing there heard this, they said, "He's calling Elijah."

Immediately one of them ran and got a sponge. He filled it with wine vinegar, put it on a staff, and offered it to Jesus to drink. The rest said, "Now leave him alone. Let's see if Elijah comes to save him."

And when Jesus had cried out again in a loud voice, he gave up his spirit.

At that moment the curtain of the temple was torn in two from top to bottom. The earth shook, the rocks split and the tombs broke open. The bodies of many holy people who had died were raised to life. They came out of the tombs after Jesus' resurrection and went into the holy city and appeared to many people.

When the centurion and those with him who were guarding Jesus saw the earthquake and all that had happened, they were terrified, and exclaimed, "Surely he was the Son of God!"

TALK ABOUT IT

- How do you think Jesus felt when everyone mocked him?
- How does Jesus respond to the people who mock him?
- Have you ever been accused of doing something you didn't actually do? How did it make you feel? How did you respond? Try and imagine what Jesus was going through.
- Does Jesus fulfill the Father's call to "act justly, love mercy, and walk humbly" in these verses? How?
- Is there anything that confuses you about this story? If so, it's okay! Do you have any questions about Matthew 27:32–54? It's time to ask your questions about the Bible.

CLOSING THOUGHT

The people who crucified Jesus and mocked him asked him to prove himself on the cross. "Save yourself!" they yelled. "Come down from the cross, if you are the Son of God." They expected Jesus to prove himself on their terms, not on God's terms. When we're challenged by someone to defend ourselves or show our worth, we usually answer that challenge by arguing, defending ourselves, or fighting back. But Jesus doesn't do that. Nothing Jesus does seems predictable.

Jesus doesn't prove he is the Son of God by saving himself—he proves he is the Son of God by saving the world. His death and resurrection shows that God is God over life *and* death.

PRAYER PROMPT

In today's verses, Jesus cries out from the cross, "My God, my God, why have you forsaken me?" It is a quote from Psalm 22:1. Do you ever feel abandoned and alone, like no one understands you? God understands that feeling. Pray through Psalm 22:1–5 (NIV) together as a family:

> My God, my God, why have you forsaken me?
>> Why are you so far from saving me,
>> so far from my cries of anguish?
> My God, I cry out by day, but you do not answer,
>> by night, but I find no rest.
>
> Yet you are enthroned as the Holy One;
>> you are the one Israel praises.
> In you our ancestors put their trust;
>> they trusted and you delivered them.
> To you they cried out and were saved;
>> in you they trusted and were not put to shame.

ACTIVITY: THE CROSS

What was meant as a punishment in Jesus's time has become a symbol of great sacrifice and love today. Draw a cross on a sheet of paper or poster board large enough so you can write on it. Take turns writing or drawing what Jesus's love and what the cross of Christ means to you. How does

Jesus treat others, and what can we do to respond the same way Jesus does in tough situations?

Four Gospels, Four Audiences

Four books in the Bible are called "The Gospels," which means, "The Good News." Each one is a different perspective on the life and teachings of Jesus. Each one was written with a different audience in mind. Think of it as if you just went on a carnival ride: you and your friend both rode the same ride, but each of you might tell about your experience a little bit differently. The ride operator in his booth and your parent standing by the exit were both watching you ride but for different reasons. They would tell the story of your ride differently too.

It's the same with the Gospels. Matthew writes to a Jewish audience, referencing many prophecies and scriptures to show how Jesus fulfills the expectation of the Messiah. Mark's Gospel is written to the Romans. As the ruling people of the day, they cared about power. This Gospel shows Jesus in action. Luke's Gospel is written to the Greeks, who loved ideas, culture, and beauty. The Gospel of Luke includes many stories, songs, and truths that would speak to the Greeks. And John's Gospel, the most unusual of the four, is written to the whole world, because the whole world needs to hear the message of love and hope that Jesus brings.

Jacob's Giant Family

SETTING UP THE STORY

During the time of Jesus, the Israelites were a huge nation of people whose numbers had grown as God had promised Abraham (see Genesis 17). Today, we're going to learn about the father of the nation of Israel—Jacob. You might remember that Abraham had two sons—Ishmael and Isaac—and that the promised blessing of a nation was to come through Isaac. (Abraham had a lot more children by other wives too.) Isaac married Rebekah and had two sons himself, twins named Jacob and Esau. In today's story, Jacob is a grown man and has left his family to find a wife.

READ: GENESIS 29:16–30:24 (MSG)

Now Laban had two daughters; Leah was the older and Rachel the younger. Leah had nice eyes, but Rachel was stunningly beautiful. And it was Rachel that Jacob loved.

So Jacob answered, "I will work for you seven years for your younger daughter Rachel."

"It is far better," said Laban, "that I give her to you than marry her to some outsider. Yes. Stay here with me."

So Jacob worked seven years for Rachel. But it only seemed like a few days, he loved her so much.

Then Jacob said to Laban, "Give me my wife; I've completed what we agreed I'd do. I'm ready to consummate my marriage." Laban invited everyone around and threw a big feast. At evening, though, he got his daughter Leah and brought her to the marriage bed, and Jacob slept with her. (Laban gave his maid Zilpah to his daughter Leah as her maid.)

Morning came: There was Leah in the marriage bed!

Jacob confronted Laban, "What have you done to me? Didn't I work all this time for the hand of Rachel? Why did you cheat me?"

"We don't do it that way in our country," said Laban. "We don't marry off the younger daughter before the older. Enjoy your week of honeymoon, and then we'll give you the other one also. But it will cost you another seven years of work."

Jacob agreed. When he'd completed the honeymoon week, Laban gave him his daughter Rachel to be his wife. (Laban gave his maid Bilhah to his daughter Rachel as her maid.) Jacob then slept with her. And he loved Rachel more than Leah. He worked for Laban another seven years.

When GOD realized that Leah was unloved, he opened her womb. But Rachel was barren. Leah became pregnant and had a son. She named him Reuben (Look-It's-a-Boy!). "This is a sign," she said, "that GOD has seen my misery; and a sign that now my husband will love me."

She became pregnant again and had another son. "GOD heard," she said, "that I was unloved and so he gave me this son also." She named this one Simeon (GOD-Heard). She became pregnant yet again—another son. She said, "Now maybe my husband will connect with me—I've given him three sons!" That's why she named him Levi (Connect). She became pregnant a final time and had a fourth son. She said, "This time I'll praise GOD." So she named him Judah (Praise-GOD). Then she stopped having children.

When Rachel realized that she wasn't having any children for Jacob, she became jealous of her sister. She told Jacob, "Give me sons or I'll die!"

Jacob got angry with Rachel and said, "Am I God? Am I the one who refused you babies?"

Rachel said, "Here's my maid Bilhah. Sleep with her. Let her substitute for me so I can have a child through her and build a family." So she gave him her maid Bilhah for a wife and Jacob slept with her. Bilhah became pregnant and gave Jacob a son.

Rachel said, "God took my side and vindicated me. He listened to me and gave me a son." She named him Dan (Vindication). Rachel's maid Bilhah became pregnant again and gave Jacob a second son. Rachel said,

"I've been in an all-out fight with my sister—and I've won." So she named him Naphtali (Fight).

When Leah saw that she wasn't having any more children, she gave her maid Zilpah to Jacob for a wife. Zilpah had a son for Jacob. Leah said, "How fortunate!" and she named him Gad (Lucky). When Leah's maid Zilpah had a second son for Jacob, Leah said, "A happy day! The women will congratulate me in my happiness." So she named him Asher (Happy).

One day during the wheat harvest Reuben found some mandrakes in the field and brought them home to his mother Leah. Rachel asked Leah, "Could I please have some of your son's mandrakes?"

Leah said, "Wasn't it enough that you got my husband away from me? And now you also want my son's mandrakes?"

Rachel said, "All right. I'll let him sleep with you tonight in exchange for your son's love-apples."

When Jacob came home that evening from the fields, Leah was there to meet him: "Sleep with me tonight; I've bartered my son's mandrakes for a night with you." So he slept with her that night. God listened to Leah; she became pregnant and gave Jacob a fifth son. She said, "God rewarded me for giving my maid to my husband." She named him Issachar (Bartered). Leah became pregnant yet again and gave Jacob a sixth son, saying, "God has given me a great gift. This time my husband will honor me with gifts—I've given him six sons!" She named him Zebulun (Honor). Last of all she had a daughter and named her Dinah.

And then God remembered Rachel. God listened to her and opened her womb. She became pregnant and had a son. She said, "God has taken away my humiliation." She named him Joseph (Add), praying, "May GOD add yet another son to me."

TALK ABOUT IT

- How long does Jacob have to wait to marry Rachel?
- Have you ever tried to do something to earn someone's love?
- Are there people in your life you envy? What are the things you are jealous for?

- Does this family seem like the type of family you would expect to be blessed by God? Why or why not?
- Is there anything that confuses you about this story? If so, it's okay! Do you have any questions about Genesis 29:16–30:24? It's time to ask your questions about the Bible.

CLOSING THOUGHT

This is a story about a blended family. There's a lot of one-upping that happens between Rachel and Leah as each tries to prove who is loved the most by Jacob. It's a strange thing to be competitive about, but in this time period in history, providing children for your husband meant everything.

God met both Leah and Rachel in their pain. Just like these women, we experience feelings of jealousy, anger, envy, and sadness. God is present through all of those emotions, helping us work through them.

PRAYER PROMPT

Pray for your family, whether big or small, blended or traditional, separated or together, that God's love might heal wounds and bring about mercies and grace to celebrate for years to come!

ACTIVITY #1: HOW DID YOUR FAMILY COME TOGETHER?

Parents, share your coming together story with the kids. Take a stroll through old photo albums and talk about how you met. Don't be afraid to share the rough parts of your journey—because that's often where we meet God the most!

ACTIVITY #2: BUILD A FAMILY TREE

Chart your family tree together, starting with your great-grandparents up to today. Parents, share some stories about your grandparents and aunts and uncles that your children might not know. What are the stories that have shaped your family's identity?

Having Children in Biblical Times

Having children—especially sons—in ancient times was important in a way that seems strange to us today. Ancient people didn't believe in a heaven or hell. They believed the only way to ensure your existence continued after your death was by having a son. A son continued a man's lifeline, and it was the woman's duty to provide her husband a son. Without children, a man and his wife were viewed as cursed by God, and having many children was viewed as being blessed by God.

Mr. Misunderstood

SETTING UP THE STORY

Last time we learned about the father of the nation of Israel, his family, and the conflict that can happen in families. In today's story, we're going to read a little about Jesus and his brothers. After Mary had Jesus, she and Joseph had other children—at least four other boys and two girls (Matthew 13:54–56). These were Jesus's half-brothers and half-sisters. Imagine growing up as the younger sibling of the Son of God! Let's read about an incident with Jesus and his brothers.

READ: JOHN 7:1–18 (NIV)

After this, Jesus went around in Galilee. He did not want to go about in Judea because the Jewish leaders there were looking for a way to kill him. But when the Jewish Festival of Tabernacles was near, Jesus' brothers said to him, "Leave Galilee and go to Judea, so that your disciples there may see the works you do. No one who wants to become a public figure acts in secret. Since you are doing these things, show yourself to the world." For even his own brothers did not believe in him.

Therefore Jesus told them, "My time is not yet here; for you any time will do. The world cannot hate you, but it hates me because I testify that its works are evil. You go to the festival. I am not going up to this festival, because my time has not yet fully come." After he had said this, he stayed in Galilee.

However, after his brothers had left for the festival, he went also, not publicly, but in secret. Now at the festival the Jewish leaders were watching for Jesus and asking, "Where is he?"

Among the crowds there was widespread whispering about him. Some said, "He is a good man."

Others replied, "No, he deceives the people." But no one would say anything publicly about him for fear of the leaders.

Not until halfway through the festival did Jesus go up to the temple courts and begin to teach. The Jews there were amazed and asked, "How did this man get such learning without having been taught?"

Jesus answered, "My teaching is not my own. It comes from the one who sent me. Anyone who chooses to do the will of God will find out whether my teaching comes from God or whether I speak on my own. Whoever speaks on their own does so to gain personal glory, but he who seeks the glory of the one who sent him is a man of truth; there is nothing false about him."

TALK ABOUT IT

- If your brother or sister started calling themselves the Son or Daughter of God, how do you think you'd react?
- Why do you think the teachers of the Law were so bothered by Jesus's teachings?
- When someone points out your faults or shortcomings, how does it make you feel?
- Have you ever formed an opinion about someone early on in your relationship, only to find out later that your opinion was wrong?
- Is there anything that confuses you about this story? If so, it's okay! Do you have any questions about John 7:1–18? It's time to ask your questions about the Bible.

CLOSING THOUGHT

Like Rachel and Leah in our story last time, there was likely jealousy and tension between Jesus and his siblings. Mary had the benefit of her experiences with the angel and the miracle of Jesus's birth to remind her of who Jesus was, but Jesus's siblings only knew him as their older brother who could do no wrong. It's no wonder they didn't understand what he was all about!

Jesus's death and resurrection changed his brother James's life. James became one of Jesus's most influential disciples, standing at the center of the early church. There is a letter by James to the church included in the Bible. And, like almost all of the early apostles, James's life was so changed by Jesus that James was killed for his beliefs. James's life proves that even the skeptical brother of Jesus can have a change of heart.

PRAYER PROMPT

It was the guys who thought they knew it all that Jesus called out as blind guides and snakes (see Matthew 23:13–39). Let's pray today that all of us, parents and children alike, would have soft hearts, humility, and space enough to let God continue to shape, change, and stretch our ideas of who he is and what he's all about in this world.

ACTIVITY: RED LIGHT, GREEN LIGHT!

When Jesus's brothers tell him to go down to the festival to step out into public office, Jesus says nope, his time hasn't come for that. But then he goes down to the festival in secret. Jesus tells the people he speaks to that his teaching isn't his own, that he and the Father are one—what God the Father says and does, so does God the Son. Play a game of red light, green light with your family. See who can follow the stop and go commands to make it to the finish line first.

Festival of Tabernacles

The festival that Jesus went to in Judea was a two-part celebration. The festival occurred in late September to late October and marked the end of the harvest season. It was also an occasion for the Jews to remember the forty years they wandered in the desert after leaving Egypt and how God was faithful to them during that time. To celebrate, the Jews camped out in tents around the temple for one week each year to remember the time in history when God made manna fall from heaven to feed the Israelites (Exodus 16) and made water spring from a rock when Moses struck it with his staff (Exodus 17:1–7). Jesus could be hinting back to that great occasion in John 7:37–38 (NIV): "On the last and greatest day of the festival, Jesus stood and said in a loud voice, 'Let anyone who is thirsty come to me and drink. Whoever believes in me, as Scripture has said, rivers of living water will flow from within them.'"

Joseph Reunited
with His Brothers

SETTING UP THE STORY

Today, we're going to find out what happened to Jacob's children. Jacob had twelve sons. Joseph was a son of Rachel and clearly Jacob's favorite. He gave Joseph special gifts that he didn't give to the others. To make matters worse, Joseph sometimes boasted in front of his brothers. The older ten grew angry at Joseph and jealous of their father's love for him.

One day they captured Joseph, sold him into slavery, and then lied to their father about it, telling Jacob that an animal had killed Joseph. At first Joseph was enslaved in Egypt, but eventually he was promoted to be leader over all of Pharaoh's wealth because he was a trustworthy worker. Meanwhile there was a severe famine, so Jacob sent Joseph's brothers to Egypt for food. They went to the leader of Pharaoh's house—Joseph—and asked for help. They didn't recognize Joseph, but Joseph recognized them!

READ: GENESIS 45 (NIV)

Then Joseph could no longer control himself before all his attendants, and he cried out, "Have everyone leave my presence!" So there was no one with Joseph when he made himself known to his brothers. And he wept so loudly that the Egyptians heard him, and Pharaoh's household heard about it.

Joseph said to his brothers, "I am Joseph! Is my father still living?" But his brothers were not able to answer him, because they were terrified at his presence.

Then Joseph said to his brothers, "Come close to me." When they had done so, he said, "I am your brother Joseph, the one you sold into Egypt! And now, do not be distressed and do not be angry with yourselves for selling me here, because it was to save lives that God sent me ahead of you. For two years now there has been famine in the land, and for the next five years there will be no plowing and reaping. But God sent me ahead of you to preserve for you a remnant on earth and to save your lives by a great deliverance.

"So then, it was not you who sent me here, but God. He made me father to Pharaoh, lord of his entire household and ruler of all Egypt. Now hurry back to my father and say to him, 'This is what your son Joseph says: God has made me lord of all Egypt. Come down to me; don't delay. You shall live in the region of Goshen and be near me—you, your children and grandchildren, your flocks and herds, and all you have. I will provide for you there, because five years of famine are still to come. Otherwise you and your household and all who belong to you will become destitute.'

"You can see for yourselves, and so can my brother Benjamin, that it is really I who am speaking to you. Tell my father about all the honor accorded me in Egypt and about everything you have seen. And bring my father down here quickly."

Then he threw his arms around his brother Benjamin and wept, and Benjamin embraced him, weeping. And he kissed all his brothers and wept over them. Afterward his brothers talked with him.

When the news reached Pharaoh's palace that Joseph's brothers had come, Pharaoh and all his officials were pleased. Pharaoh said to Joseph, "Tell your brothers, 'Do this: Load your animals and return to the land of Canaan, and bring your father and your families back to me. I will give you the best of the land of Egypt and you can enjoy the fat of the land.'

"You are also directed to tell them, 'Do this: Take some carts from Egypt for your children and your wives, and get your father and come. Never mind about your belongings, because the best of all Egypt will be yours.'"

So the sons of Israel did this. Joseph gave them carts, as Pharaoh had commanded, and he also gave them provisions for their journey. To each of them he gave new clothing, but to Benjamin he gave three hundred shekels of silver and five sets of clothes. And this is what he sent to his father: ten donkeys loaded with the best things of Egypt, and ten female donkeys loaded with grain and bread and other provisions for his journey.

Then he sent his brothers away, and as they were leaving he said to them, "Don't quarrel on the way!"

So they went up out of Egypt and came to their father Jacob in the land of Canaan. They told him, "Joseph is still alive! In fact, he is ruler of all Egypt." Jacob was stunned; he did not believe them. But when they told him everything Joseph had said to them, and when he saw the carts Joseph had sent to carry him back, the spirit of their father Jacob revived. And Israel said, "I'm convinced! My son Joseph is still alive. I will go and see him before I die."

TALK ABOUT IT

- If you were Joseph in this story, what would you have done when the brothers arrived?
- How do you think Joseph's brothers felt when they found out it was Joseph, the brother they had sold into slavery, who was in power in Egypt?
- What are some other ways Joseph could have responded to his brothers?
- What does Joseph have to say about God in this story?
- Is there anything that confuses you about this story? If so, it's okay! Do you have any questions about Genesis 45? It's time to ask your questions about the Bible.

CLOSING THOUGHT

This story could have turned out so many different ways. If Joseph had been more vengeful, he could have sent his brothers away without food. He was in a great position of power; it's even possible he could have had them imprisoned for what they had done to him. And yet, because of the good work that God had given Joseph to do, Joseph was able to see God's hand in all of it, the good things and the bad. Joseph reassured his brothers: "Don't be afraid. Am I in the place of God? You intended to harm me, but God intended it for good to accomplish what is now being done, the saving of many lives" (Genesis 50:19–20 NIV).

That is the power of God. He is in the business of taking our hurts, our selfishness, and the wrongs of the world and making beautiful things happen.

PRAYER PROMPT

Are there times in your family's life that have been really hard or painful? In what ways has that experience been redeemed by God? Can you see the light, even in the darkness? Pray that God would heal those hurts, and thank God for the ways he is already working or has worked to bring about good through that tough experience.

ACTIVITY: MEAL MATCH

Because of Joseph's access to wealth and resources, he was able to provide food to his brothers in need. Choose a way your family can provide food for someone else this week. Here are some ideas: instead of eating out one night, use the money you would have spent to buy food for a shelter or food bank. Make a meal for someone you know who could use that blessing. Buy a gift card for a restaurant and send it to a friend or family member. If you're eating out or going through the drive-thru, pay the tab of the customer behind you. Or come up with your own way to show love through food this week!

Israelites in Egypt

When Joseph's brothers sold him into slavery, they could never have imagined all that God had in store for Joseph, their family, and the future nation of Israel. Joseph's diligent work in Egypt drew his family to Egypt during the years of famine. His family members were descendants of Abraham. As years passed in Egypt, more and more children were born and Joseph's family eventually grew into the nation of Israel.

The book of Genesis ends with the people of Israel in Egypt as a free people. When Joseph's generation died, the next Pharaoh had no connection to the Israelites, so as their tribes grew, the Egyptians felt threatened. The Egyptians oppressed and enslaved the people of Israel. When the people of Israel cried out to their God, he heard, and he answered.

I Am Who I Am

SETTING UP THE STORY

There are about three hundred years between the nation of Israel set-tling in Egypt at the end of Genesis (Joseph's story) and Pharaoh feeling threatened by the Israelites at the beginning of Exodus. That's a big span of time. Think about what was happening in history three hundred years ago from our present day. The entire world has changed, right? Watch out, God is doing a new thing!

READ: EXODUS 3–4:17 (MSG)

Moses was shepherding the flock of Jethro, his father-in-law, the priest of Midian. He led the flock to the west end of the wilderness and came to the mountain of God, Horeb. The angel of GOD appeared to him in flames of fire blazing out of the middle of a bush. He looked. The bush was blazing away but it didn't burn up.

Moses said, "What's going on here? I can't believe this! Amazing! Why doesn't the bush burn up?"

GOD saw that he had stopped to look. God called to him from out of the bush, "Moses! Moses!"

He said, "Yes? I'm right here!"

God said, "Don't come any closer. Remove your sandals from your feet. You're standing on holy ground."

Then he said, "I am the God of your father: The God of Abraham, the God of Isaac, the God of Jacob."

Moses hid his face, afraid to look at God.

GOD said, "I've taken a good, long look at the affliction of my people in Egypt. I've heard their cries for deliverance from their slave masters; I know all about their pain. And now I have come down to help them, pry them loose from the grip of Egypt, get them out of that country and bring them to a good land with wide-open spaces, a land lush with milk and honey, the land of the Canaanite, the Hittite, the Amorite, the Perizzite, the Hivite, and the Jebusite.

"The Israelite cry for help has come to me, and I've seen for myself how cruelly they're being treated by the Egyptians. It's time for you to go back: I'm sending you to Pharaoh to bring my people, the People of Israel, out of Egypt."

Moses answered God, "But why me? What makes you think that I could ever go to Pharaoh and lead the children of Israel out of Egypt?"

"I'll be with you," God said. "And this will be the proof that I am the one who sent you: When you have brought my people out of Egypt, you will worship God right here at this very mountain."

Then Moses said to God, "Suppose I go to the People of Israel and I tell them, 'The God of your fathers sent me to you'; and they ask me, 'What is his name?' What do I tell them?"

God said to Moses, "I-AM-WHO-I-AM. Tell the People of Israel, 'I-AM sent me to you.'"

God continued with Moses: "This is what you're to say to the Israelites: 'GOD, the God of your fathers, the God of Abraham, the God of Isaac, and the God of Jacob sent me to you.' This has always been my name, and this is how I always will be known.

"Now be on your way. Gather the leaders of Israel. Tell them, 'GOD, the God of your fathers, the God of Abraham, Isaac, and Jacob, appeared to me, saying, "I've looked into what's being done to you in Egypt, and I've determined to get you out of the affliction of Egypt and take you to the land of the Canaanite, the Hittite, the Amorite, the Perizzite, the Hivite, and the Jebusite, a land brimming over with milk and honey."'

"Believe me, they will listen to you. Then you and the leaders of Israel will go to the king of Egypt and say to him: 'GOD, the God of the Hebrews, has met with us. Let us take a three-day journey into the wilderness where we will worship GOD—*our* God.'

"I know that the king of Egypt won't let you go unless forced to, so I'll intervene and hit Egypt where it hurts—oh, my miracles will send them reeling!—after which they'll be glad to send you off. I'll see to it that this people get a hearty send-off by the Egyptians—when you leave, you won't leave empty-handed! Each woman will ask her neighbor and any guests in her house for objects of silver and gold, for jewelry and extra clothes; you'll put them on your sons and daughters. Oh, you'll clean the Egyptians out!"

Moses objected, "They won't trust me. They won't listen to a word I say. They're going to say, 'GOD? Appear to him? Hardly!'"

So GOD said, "What's that in your hand?"

"A staff."

"Throw it on the ground." He threw it. It became a snake; Moses jumped back—fast!

GOD said to Moses, "Reach out and grab it by the tail." He reached out and grabbed it—and he was holding his staff again. "That's so they will trust that GOD appeared to you, the God of their fathers, the God of Abraham, the God of Isaac, and the God of Jacob."

GOD then said, "Put your hand inside your shirt." He slipped his hand under his shirt, then took it out. His hand had turned leprous, like snow.

He said, "Put your hand back under your shirt." He did it, then took it back out—as healthy as before.

"So if they don't trust you and aren't convinced by the first sign, the second sign should do it. But if it doesn't, if even after these two signs they don't trust you and listen to your message, take some water out of the Nile and pour it out on the dry land; the Nile water that you pour out will turn to blood when it hits the ground."

Moses raised another objection to GOD: "Master, please, I don't talk well. I've never been good with words, neither before nor after you spoke to me. I stutter and stammer."

GOD said, "And who do you think made the human mouth? And who makes some mute, some deaf, some sighted, some blind? Isn't it I, GOD? So, get going. I'll be right there with you—with your mouth! I'll be right there to teach you what to say."

He said, "Oh, Master, please! Send somebody else!"

GOD got angry with Moses: "Don't you have a brother, Aaron the Levite? He's good with words, I know he is. He speaks very well. In fact, at this very moment he's on his way to meet you. When he sees you he's going to be glad. You'll speak to him and tell him what to say. I'll be right there with you as you speak and with him as he speaks, teaching you step by step. He will speak to the people for you. He'll act as your mouth, but you'll decide what comes out of it. Now take this staff in your hand; you'll use it to do the signs."

TALK ABOUT IT

- If you saw a bush on fire and it started talking to you, what would you do? What would you say?
- What does God ask Moses to do?
- How does Moses respond?
- What are some reasons Moses doesn't want to follow through with God's plan?
- Have you ever felt someone was asking you to do far more than you ever thought you could? How did you feel?
- What are some of the ways God addressed Moses's fears?
- Close your eyes and try to imagine these things: your walking stick becomes a snake, and your hand shrivels up. Describe what you see.
- Is there anything that confuses you about this story? If so, it's okay! Do you have any questions about Exodus 3–4:17? It's time to ask your questions about the Bible.

CLOSING THOUGHT

You'd think if you encountered a talking bush on fire in the middle of the desert, there'd be no questioning that voice—*yes sir, no sir, absolutely sir*—but that's not what happened here. Moses begged God, argued with God, and just about said *no thanks* to God.

But in this story we see God's love and patience in a new way. God met Moses in his doubts. First God said, "I will be with you." Then he said, "I AM WHO I AM," which means "You can trust that I will be with you because I am exactly who I say that I am—God." Then God told Moses that he'd be able to know that he was still walking with God by the miraculous things that would happen as they walked together.

God can cause amazing things to happen in our relationships and in our world when we follow him. Some of these things can be truly miraculous, like staffs turning into snakes, hands being healed, and water turning into blood.

PRAYER PROMPT

It takes courage in our everyday calling to be God's people. Thank God for his promise to be with you each day. Ask God to remind you who he is and what he's all about. And praise God for the ways he works through you and your relationships.

ACTIVITY: FIRE!

If you have access to one, plan a night to have a fire, either in a backyard fire pit or in your living room fireplace. If you can't build a fire where you live, stake out a pretend campfire ring in your living room and have a campout! Tell stories of times when God has been with you.

Moses's Early Life

Moses was in the desert when we met him today because of what had happened to him earlier in his life. Moses grew up in both the Jewish and the Egyptian worlds, in a time when there was hatred toward the Israelites. He was adopted by Pharaoh's daughter and grew up in Pharaoh's court. Moses's early life positioned him to speak to Pharaoh on behalf of the Israelites. God has a way of using the circumstances of our lives to shape our characters and to achieve a greater good. He does this with Moses, who seems like just the man for the job, even if Moses has his fears and doubts.

Blood, Frogs, Darkness, and Hardened Hearts

SETTING UP THE STORY

Moses decided to follow God's calling and go back to Egypt to talk to Pharaoh. Moses only asked Pharaoh for a few days in the wilderness so the Israelites could worship God, but Pharaoh relied too much on the Israelites as slaves and couldn't imagine letting them go, even for a couple of days. Instead, he increased their work. The Israelites felt oppressed and cried out to God (Exodus 5). What takes place over the next few chapters of Exodus is a war of the gods, with the God of the Hebrews demonstrating his power and might against the gods of Egypt. God sends plagues each time Pharaoh says no to Moses's plea to "Let my people go" (read Exodus 7–10 to learn more about the plagues). It all comes to a head in this final moment.

READ: EXODUS 11:1–10 (NLT)

Then the LORD said to Moses, "I will strike Pharaoh and the land of Egypt with one more blow. After that, Pharaoh will let you leave this country. In fact, he will be so eager to get rid of you that he will force you all to leave. Tell all the Israelite men and women to ask their Egyptian neighbors for articles of silver and gold." (Now the LORD had caused the Egyptians to look favorably on the people of Israel. And Moses was considered a very great man in the land of Egypt, respected by Pharaoh's officials and the Egyptian people alike.)

Moses had announced to Pharaoh, "This is what the LORD says: At midnight tonight I will pass through the heart of Egypt. All the firstborn sons will die in every family in Egypt, from the oldest son of Pharaoh, who sits on his throne, to the oldest son of his lowliest servant girl who grinds the flour. Even the firstborn of all the livestock will die. Then a loud wail will rise throughout the land of Egypt, a wail like no one has heard before or will ever hear again. But among the Israelites it will be so peaceful that not even a dog will bark. Then you will know that the LORD makes a distinction between the Egyptians and the Israelites. All the officials of Egypt will run to me and fall to the ground before me. 'Please leave!' they will beg. 'Hurry! And take all your followers with you.' Only then will I go!" Then, burning with anger, Moses left Pharaoh.

Now the LORD had told Moses earlier, "Pharaoh will not listen to you, but then I will do even more mighty miracles in the land of Egypt." Moses and Aaron performed these miracles in Pharaoh's presence, but the LORD hardened Pharaoh's heart, and he wouldn't let the Israelites leave the country.

TALK ABOUT IT
- Why do you think Moses was so angry when he left Pharaoh?
- Do you ever drag your feet doing something because it isn't what you want to do?
- Why do you think Pharaoh was so hard to convince, even with such a huge warning from Moses, to let the Israelites leave Egypt?
- What do you think it means to have a "hardened heart"?
- Is there anything that confuses you about this story? If so, it's okay! Do you have any questions about Exodus 11:1–10? It's time to ask your questions about the Bible.

CLOSING THOUGHT
People throughout history have oppressed other people for their own gain. God speaks time and time again against the oppression of people. When people are oppressed like the Israelites in the story, God hears that cry.

The exodus story shows how the Israelites' God was greater and more powerful than the gods around them. The God of Israel just keeps showing us how different he is. He freed a nation of slaves from a powerful ruling nation and their false gods. When Jesus arrived on the scene about fifteen hundred years after the exodus story, he didn't just prove that he was greater and more powerful than the false religion of his day, he redefined entirely what greatness and power look like. Where other leaders pushed down the weak and vulnerable, Jesus listened, protected, and taught. Where other leaders tortured and killed people to prove their might, Jesus healed and rescued.

PRAYER PROMPT

Pray that God would help keep our hearts soft to the weak, the oppressed, and the hurting. Ask God to show you if you've been taking advantage of a friend or family member, and if so, ask for and receive his or her forgiveness. Pray for God's Holy Spirit to bring about a spirit of kindness and love in your relationships.

ACTIVITY: RANDOM ACTS OF KINDNESS

Pharaoh demanded a lot from the Israelites, but our God does not require major sacrifices—just humility, mercy, and justice. This week, look for opportunities to be kind to others. Help out around the house without being asked, hold open doors for people, or just say a kind word—you decide how you want to practice being kind, and then just go and do it! Share with your family the ways you practiced being kind daily throughout the week.

The Gods of Egypt

Egyptians worshipped many gods. Pharaoh was understood by the Egyptians as the gods' representative on earth. When God sent the plagues, they were direct attacks to show the Egyptians his power over the many gods they worshipped. The Nile River turning to blood demonstrated God's power over the Egyptians' source of life. The Egyptian goddess of fertility had the head of a frog, so God sent tons of frogs out of the Nile. When God caused the world to become dark, it was to show how God is more powerful than the most high Egyptian sun god, Ra, the father of Pharaoh. By the end of the plagues, God had established himself as the One True God above all others.

Jesus Turns Water into Wine

SETTING UP THE STORY

Last time we learned about the plagues that God brought on Egypt to defeat Pharaoh's gods. One of them was turning the Nile River from water to blood. Today, we're going to read about another miracle involving water, only this time it's about Jesus. This story takes place about three years *before* Jesus died on the cross.

READ: JOHN 2:1–12 (NRSV)

On the third day there was a wedding in Cana of Galilee, and the mother of Jesus was there. Jesus and his disciples had also been invited to the wedding. When the wine gave out, the mother of Jesus said to him, "They have no wine."

And Jesus said to her, "Woman, what concern is that to you and to me? My hour has not yet come." His mother said to the servants, "Do whatever he tells you."

Now standing there were six stone water jars for the Jewish rites of purification, each holding twenty or thirty gallons. Jesus said to them, "Fill the jars with water." And they filled them up to the brim. He said to them, "Now draw some out, and take it to the chief steward." So they took it. When the steward tasted the water that had become wine, and did not know where it came from (though the servants who had drawn the water knew), the steward called the bridegroom and said to him, "Everyone serves the good wine first, and then the inferior wine after the guests have become drunk. But you have kept the good wine until now."

Jesus did this, the first of his signs, in Cana of Galilee, and revealed his glory; and his disciples believed in him.

After this he went down to Capernaum with his mother, his brothers, and his disciples; and they remained there a few days.

TALK ABOUT IT

- Why do you think Jesus's mother told him there was no more wine at the wedding?
- What's your favorite treat at a party?
- How would you feel if that treat was all gone before you got some?
- How would you feel if suddenly there were more of your favorite kind of treat, a ton of it, and it was the best kind of treat ever?
- Why do you think people tell this story about Jesus at the wedding?
- Why do you think it matters that Jesus saved the best wine until the end of the wedding? What does this tell us about who he is?
- Is there anything that confuses you about this story? If so, it's okay! Do you have any questions about John 2:1–12? It's time to ask your questions about the Bible.

CLOSING THOUGHT

Jesus used water from six stone jars that were used by the Jews to keep the purity laws of the Old Testament. The Jews had set up all kinds of laws and rituals to try to keep themselves pure before God so that he would find them acceptable and bless them.

Only that isn't how God works.

Jesus transformed what was used by people to try to please God into wine, which symbolized sustenance and life. It represented God's giant promise to his people (a covenant) to bless all people. And wine meant celebration, joy, and festivities. When Jesus changed water that was meant for ceremonial cleansing into wine, he turned over the whole system of obeying the law in order to earn God's love!

PRAYER PROMPT

The miracle at Cana reminds us that God has power over heaven and earth and that he draws all things back to himself. Pray together Psalm 104, a psalm of praise for God the Creator!

ACTIVITY #1: HOOP JUMPING

Create an obstacle course around your home or your yard. Time each other to see how long it takes you to get through the course. After you've each gone through the obstacle course, clear the route and time yourself running as fast as you can to the finish line. God doesn't set up obstacles for you to get to his love, so sprint toward God's love with all your might, kiddos!

ACTIVITY #2: TOAST TO YOUR FAMILY AND GOD'S LOVE

Choose a night this week to prepare a special meal with your family (bonus points if you help Mom or Dad make the food). Buy a bottle of sparkling grape juice or ginger ale. Before the meal, pour everyone a special glass of bubbly and share a toast of God's abundant grace, mercy, and love.

Numbers in the Bible

Numbers carried a lot of meaning for the people in the Bible. Anytime a specific number is given, you can bet there's a reason why that number is there. In this story today, the miracle at Cana took place "on the third day." Three is a number of completeness. People in biblical times would have known that this meant Jesus fulfilled—or completed—the law.

Another number—six—appears in this story. There are six stone water jars, and six meant incomplete, weak, or not of God. Early readers of this story would have seen this number and realized the writer of the story was calling the purity rituals in the Law incomplete, unnecessary, or made by humans and not by God.

Keep watch for other numbers in the Bible and you'll find all kinds of clues about what the writers of the Bible want you to know!

Moses and Passover

SETTING UP THE STORY

In ancient times, tribal stories of gods engaging in epic battles sometimes helped to explain how and why certain events happened. Through the Holy Spirit, the ancient writers of the Bible recorded their history in the same way. How did the tribal nation of Israel escape Egypt? By the One True God demonstrating his power over the gods of Egypt (Exodus 12:12). As we return to the story of Moses, remember how the Egyptians were oppressing the people of Israel, and Pharaoh was unwilling to let them leave to worship God? Because of this unwillingness, God sent plagues against the Egyptians and their gods. The passage we read today is central to Israel's story as well as our own faith story.

READ: EXODUS 12:21–42 (MSG)

Moses assembled all the elders of Israel. He said, "Select a lamb for your families and slaughter the Passover lamb. Take a bunch of hyssop and dip it in the bowl of blood and smear it on the lintel and on the two door-posts. No one is to leave the house until morning. GOD will pass through to strike Egypt down. When he sees the blood on the lintel and the two doorposts, GOD will pass over the doorway; he won't let the destroyer enter your house to strike you down with ruin.

"Keep this word. It's the law for you and your children, forever. When you enter the land which GOD will give you as he promised, keep doing this. And when your children say to you, 'Why are we doing this?' tell them: 'It's the Passover-sacrifice to GOD who passed over the homes of the Israelites in Egypt when he hit Egypt with death but rescued us.'"

The people bowed and worshiped.

The Israelites then went and did what GOD had commanded Moses and Aaron. They did it all.

At midnight GOD struck every firstborn in the land of Egypt, from the firstborn of Pharaoh, who sits on his throne, right down to the firstborn of the prisoner locked up in jail. Also the firstborn of the animals.

Pharaoh got up that night, he and all his servants and everyone else in Egypt—what wild wailing and lament in Egypt! There wasn't a house in which someone wasn't dead.

Pharaoh called in Moses and Aaron that very night and said, "Get out of here and be done with you—you and your Israelites! Go worship GOD on your own terms. And yes, take your sheep and cattle as you've insisted, but go. And bless me."

The Egyptians couldn't wait to get rid of them; they pushed them to hurry up, saying, "We're all as good as dead."

The people grabbed their bread dough before it had risen, bundled their bread bowls in their cloaks and threw them over their shoulders. The Israelites had already done what Moses had told them; they had asked the Egyptians for silver and gold things and clothing. GOD saw to it that the Egyptians liked the people and so readily gave them what they asked for. Oh yes! They picked those Egyptians clean.

The Israelites moved on from Rameses to Succoth, about 600,000 on foot, besides their dependents. There was also a crowd of riffraff tagging along, not to mention the large flocks and herds of livestock. They baked unraised cakes with the bread dough they had brought out of Egypt; it hadn't raised—they'd been rushed out of Egypt and hadn't time to fix food for the journey.

The Israelites had lived in Egypt 430 years. At the end of the 430 years, to the very day, God's entire army left Egypt. God kept watch all night, watching over the Israelites as he brought them out of Egypt. Because God kept watch, all Israel for all generations will honor God by keeping watch this night—a watchnight.

TALK ABOUT IT

- How did God tell Moses and Aaron he would protect the Israelites?
- After all of the plagues the Egyptians have faced, is Pharaoh's heart still hard?

- Why do you think the Israelites were in a rush to leave Egypt?
- A lot of children died in Egypt on this day. What do you think about that?
- How do you think the Israelites felt in this story? How about the Egyptians? How about Pharaoh?
- Is there anything that confuses you about this story? If so, it's okay! Do you have any questions about Exodus 12:21–42? It's time to ask your questions about the Bible.

CLOSING THOUGHT

The Israelites' freedom from Egypt marks the beginning of a new era for the nation of Israel. After spending four hundred years in slavery, the Israelites have finally been released, and God has shown his strength as the One True God against the Egyptians' gods. The Lord heard the cries of the oppressed and declared them free!

Knowing what we know about God through Jesus Christ, it's hard to imagine our God killing the firstborn of every Egyptian in order to prove he's awesome. But just like the story of Noah and the flood, it's important to remember that these stories were how the people of Israel made sense of the world. Tribal nations everywhere saw the gods as angry, impatient, jealous, and wrathful. But our God changed the way his people saw him. He showed them his protection and commitment to them, his mercy and his salvation. No other god in ancient times was known to be like that.

As followers of Christ, the Passover story is central to our own understanding of who God is. John the Baptist called Jesus the Lamb of God, sent to take away the sins of the world (John 1:29). We'll learn more about that next time.

PRAYER PROMPT

There are many ways we can feel oppressed. We can be anxious, worried, stressed, or angry. We can be consumed with a desire to be perfect and to follow the rules at the expense of relationships. We can be enslaved to our passions, addictions, and selfish desires. We can be oppressed by other people. God meets us in all of our chains and frees us from that oppression.

This story shows us that God hears, comforts, and provides. Pray that God would reveal to you and your family ways out of darkness so that you can each experience the light of his freedom, love, and grace.

ACTIVITY: CELEBRATE PASSOVER

Even if it isn't near the actual holiday, you can plan a Passover meal to commemorate the journey from slavery to freedom. Each of the foods and rituals of the feast have meaning. With your parents' permission, search the internet for "cooking a Passover meal at home." You'll find lots of good ideas.

Why a Lamb?

The Israelites were told to sacrifice a lamb for a very specific reason. Remember how this story is about a war between the One True God of Israel and the Egyptian gods? One of the Egyptian gods, Amun, was seen as the king of the gods. Amun had the head of a ram (or male sheep),[5] so the Egyptians considered sheep to be a sacred animal and wouldn't eat or slaughter it. When God told the Israelites to sacrifice sheep in the presence of the Egyptians, it was a symbol of how the one true God is stronger than Amun.

Jesus's Last Supper and Our Communion

SETTING UP THE STORY

Last time we learned about Passover, the Jewish celebration of God rescuing Israel from Egypt. The Passover became an annual feast that was practiced by the Israelites for at least eight hundred years before Jesus. It reminded the Israelites of God's promises, that he is a protector and rescuer. Jesus also celebrated Passover, which happened to be his last supper before his crucifixion.

READ: LUKE 22:7–20 (NLT)

Now the Festival of Unleavened Bread arrived, when the Passover lamb is sacrificed. Jesus sent Peter and John ahead and said, "Go and prepare the Passover meal, so we can eat it together."

"Where do you want us to prepare it?" they asked him.

He replied, "As soon as you enter Jerusalem, a man carrying a pitcher of water will meet you. Follow him. At the house he enters, say to the owner, 'The Teacher asks: Where is the guest room where I can eat the Passover meal with my disciples?' He will take you upstairs to a large room that is already set up. That is where you should prepare our meal." They went off to the city and found everything just as Jesus had said, and they prepared the Passover meal there.

When the time came, Jesus and the apostles sat down together at the table. Jesus said, "I have been very eager to eat this Passover meal with you before my suffering begins. For I tell you now that I won't eat this meal again until its meaning is fulfilled in the Kingdom of God."

Then he took a cup of wine and gave thanks to God for it. Then he said, "Take this and share it among yourselves. For I will not drink wine again until the Kingdom of God has come."

He took some bread and gave thanks to God for it. Then he broke it in pieces and gave it to the disciples, saying, "This is my body, which is given for you. Do this in remembrance of me."

After supper he took another cup of wine and said, "This cup is the new covenant between God and his people—an agreement confirmed with my blood, which is poured out as a sacrifice for you."

TALK ABOUT IT

- What do you think Jesus meant by his "suffering"?
- What do you think Jesus means when he says the wine is his blood and the bread is his body?
- Does your family have traditions at church, at home, or around the holidays?
- Why do you think you keep doing those things?
- Why do you think Jesus used this important, traditional celebration meal to talk about his death?
- Is there anything that confuses you about this story? If so, it's okay! Do you have any questions about Luke 22:7–20? It's time to ask your questions about the Bible.

CLOSING THOUGHT

The Passover meal takes place right before Jesus is arrested and crucified. For centuries, the Jews had been remembering how God rescued them from captivity and oppression through the Passover meal. Now, in the midst of such an important feast, Jesus redefined Passover for his disciples, the Jews, and anyone who followed him.

Before, Passover meant God rescued the Jews. Now, Passover means God rescues *everyone*—all people—through Jesus.

We remember Jesus's love, mercy, and forgiveness today through the practice of Communion or the Eucharist. Taking communion varies depending on your church's history and traditions, but no matter what way you take communion, and no matter what you call it, it started here, with

Jesus and his disciples. Before, the Jews celebrated the Passover by roasting a lamb to represent the blood of the lamb that saved them in Egypt. Jesus changed that practice. As the Lamb of God himself, he said every time we eat bread or drink wine, we should remember his love and sacrifice. God's love is big!

PRAYER PROMPT: PRAY THROUGH PSALM 25 (NLT)

O Lord, I give my life to you.
　　I trust in you, my God!
Do not let me be disgraced,
　　or let my enemies rejoice in my defeat.
No one who trusts in you will ever be disgraced,
　　but disgrace comes to those who try to deceive others.

Show me the right path, O Lord;
　　point out the road for me to follow.
Lead me by your truth and teach me,
　　for you are the God who saves me.
　　All day long I put my hope in you.
Remember, O Lord, your compassion and unfailing love,
　　which you have shown from long ages past.
Do not remember the rebellious sins of my youth.
　　Remember me in the light of your unfailing love,
　　for you are merciful, O Lord.

The Lord is good and does what is right;
　　he shows the proper path to those who go astray.
He leads the humble in doing right,
　　teaching them his way.
The Lord leads with unfailing love and faithfulness
　　all who keep his covenant and obey his demands.

For the honor of your name, O Lord,
　　forgive my many, many sins.

Who are those who fear the LORD?
> He will show them the path they should choose.
They will live in prosperity,
> and their children will inherit the land.
The LORD is a friend to those who fear him.
> He teaches them his covenant.
My eyes are always on the LORD,
> for he rescues me from the traps of my enemies.

Turn to me and have mercy,
> for I am alone and in deep distress.
My problems go from bad to worse.
> Oh, save me from them all!
Feel my pain and see my trouble.
> Forgive all my sins.
See how many enemies I have
> and how viciously they hate me!
Protect me! Rescue my life from them!
> Do not let me be disgraced, for in you I take refuge.
May integrity and honesty protect me,
> for I put my hope in you.

O God, ransom Israel
> from all its troubles.

ACTIVITY: FAMILY COMMUNION

Get grape juice or wine and a loaf of bread and serve each other communion. Before you eat together, talk about the things that you love most about Jesus. What are some of your favorite things about God? Before you drink together, take turns thanking God for what you just named. You can make a habit at any meal of remembering Jesus in this way too!

Four Cups of Passover

During the traditional Passover meal, four cups are served. Each cup is given to remember one of God's promises, written in Exodus 6:6–7 (NLT): "Therefore, say to the people of Israel: 'I am the Lord. (1) I will free you from your oppression and (2) will rescue you from your slavery in Egypt. (3) I will redeem you with a powerful arm and great acts of judgment. (4) I will claim you as my own people, and I will be your God. Then you will know that I am the Lord your God who has freed you from your oppression in Egypt." In today's story, Jesus tells us *he* is the one who will fulfill the four promises of God for all people through his sacrifice. He also put his own blessing on a cup of wine.

The Cloud, the Fire, and the Water

SETTING UP THE STORY

After the final plague hit Egypt and wiped out every firstborn, you would think that would've been the end of Pharaoh's relationship with Israel, but that isn't the case. Let's read about what happens with Moses and the Israelites after they fled Egypt.

READ: EXODUS 13:21–22, 14:5–31 (NIV)

By day the LORD went ahead of them in a pillar of cloud to guide them on their way and by night in a pillar of fire to give them light, so that they could travel by day or night. Neither the pillar of cloud by day nor the pillar of fire by night left its place in front of the people. . . .

When the king of Egypt was told that the people had fled, Pharaoh and his officials changed their minds about them and said, "What have we done? We have let the Israelites go and have lost their services!" So he had his chariot made ready and took his army with him. He took six hundred of the best chariots, along with all the other chariots of Egypt, with officers over all of them. The LORD hardened the heart of Pharaoh king of Egypt, so that he pursued the Israelites, who were marching out boldly. The Egyptians—all Pharaoh's horses and chariots, horsemen and troops—pursued the Israelites and overtook them as they camped by the sea near Pi Hahiroth, opposite Baal Zephon.

As Pharaoh approached, the Israelites looked up, and there were the Egyptians, marching after them. They were terrified and cried out to the LORD. They said to Moses, "Was it because there were no graves in Egypt that you brought us to the desert to die? What have you done to us by bringing us out of Egypt? Didn't we say to you in Egypt, 'Leave us alone;

let us serve the Egyptians'? It would have been better for us to serve the Egyptians than to die in the desert!"

Moses answered the people, "Do not be afraid. Stand firm and you will see the deliverance the LORD will bring you today. The Egyptians you see today you will never see again. The LORD will fight for you; you need only to be still."

Then the LORD said to Moses, "Why are you crying out to me? Tell the Israelites to move on. Raise your staff and stretch out your hand over the sea to divide the water so that the Israelites can go through the sea on dry ground. I will harden the hearts of the Egyptians so that they will go in after them. And I will gain glory through Pharaoh and all his army, through his chariots and his horsemen. The Egyptians will know that I am the LORD when I gain glory through Pharaoh, his chariots and his horsemen."

Then the angel of God, who had been traveling in front of Israel's army, withdrew and went behind them. The pillar of cloud also moved from in front and stood behind them, coming between the armies of Egypt and Israel. Throughout the night the cloud brought darkness to the one side and light to the other side; so neither went near the other all night long.

Then Moses stretched out his hand over the sea, and all that night the LORD drove the sea back with a strong east wind and turned it into dry land. The waters were divided, and the Israelites went through the sea on dry ground, with a wall of water on their right and on their left.

The Egyptians pursued them, and all Pharaoh's horses and chariots and horsemen followed them into the sea. During the last watch of the night the LORD looked down from the pillar of fire and cloud at the Egyptian army and threw it into confusion. He jammed the wheels of their chariots so that they had difficulty driving. And the Egyptians said, "Let's get away from the Israelites! The LORD is fighting for them against Egypt."

Then the LORD said to Moses, "Stretch out your hand over the sea so that the waters may flow back over the Egyptians and their chariots and horsemen." Moses stretched out his hand over the sea, and at daybreak the sea went back to its place. The Egyptians were fleeing toward it, and the LORD swept them into the sea. The water flowed back and covered the chariots and horsemen—the entire army of Pharaoh that had followed the Israelites into the sea. Not one of them survived.

But the Israelites went through the sea on dry ground, with a wall of water on their right and on their left. That day the LORD saved Israel from the hands of the Egyptians, and Israel saw the Egyptians lying dead on the shore. And when the Israelites saw the mighty hand of the LORD displayed against the Egyptians, the people feared the LORD and put their trust in him and in Moses his servant.

TALK ABOUT IT
- What is the Israelites' reaction to being pursued by Pharaoh and his army?
- What are some ways that God takes care of the Israelites in this story?
- How crazy is it that God split a sea in half? Do you think anyone—a person, an army, *anyone*—could do that today?
- Talk about a time when you've been afraid. How have you overcome that fear?
- How does God help the Israelites overcome their fears?
- Is there anything that confuses you about this story? If so, it's okay! Do you have any questions about Exodus 13:21–22, 14:5–31? It's time to ask your questions about the Bible.

CLOSING THOUGHT
The Israelites just spent four hundred years in Egypt, oppressed by Pharaoh. In a quick season of miracles, God heard their cry and rescued them from their oppressors. But now the oppressors are approaching fast, and it's no wonder the Israelites are afraid that God might not come through, even though he's come through all of the times before.

God's kryptonite for fear is love. In this story, God shows his love and protection by surrounding the Israelites with a pillar of cloud by day and a pillar of fire by night. God opens up the sea to guide the Israelites to the other side. And God will continue to do even more miraculous things.

PRAYER PROMPT

After Pharaoh and his army get washed away in the sea, Miriam (Moses's sister) and Moses sing a song about the victory, including these lines from Exodus 15:2 (NIV):

> The LORD is my strength and my defense;
>> he has become my salvation.
> He is my God, and I will praise him,
>> my father's God, and I will exalt him.

The "song of the sea" is one of the oldest surviving texts describing the Exodus, possibly written as many as three thousand years ago. It has been sung, read, and repeated by millions of followers of God. Join your voices together with that chorus! Take turns reading these lines and then pray the poem together.

ACTIVITY: THE TRAVELING STORY

The song you prayed today is written in a much older version of Hebrew (the original language of the Old Testament) than even the verses surrounding it. In the Bible, different writers' stories are woven together to tell a bigger story of God's love.

Take turns building on a story of strength and protection. Start with one line and then work your way through each person in your family, each adding a line to the story. You can create your own story, or try to retell the story of Moses and the Israelites.

With Timbrels and Dancing

After Moses and the Israelites cross the sea on dry ground, all of Israel rejoices in song, led by Moses and Miriam. Exodus 15:20 (NIV) says, "Then Miriam the prophet, Aaron's sister, took a timbrel in her hand, and all the women followed her, with timbrels and dancing." (A *timbrel* is a tambourine-type instrument.) Miriam was the big sister of both Aaron and Moses, thought to be five years older than Moses and three years older than Aaron. She is the one who rescued Moses when he was an infant, and she walks closely with Aaron and Moses throughout the Exodus account. The Talmud (a very important Jewish text) counts Miriam as one of the seven major female prophets of Israel.

Faith for the Waves

SETTING UP THE STORY

Last time we saw how God mastered the sea and allowed the Israelites to cross through the waters and escape the Egyptians without being harmed. Fast forward fifteen hundred years to Jesus's time, and once again we'll see God demonstrate his power and his might. Earlier in the day in today's story, Jesus had spent a lot of time teaching his disciples about the kingdom of God through parables, or stories that help listeners uncover deeper truths. Jesus is about to teach the disciples another lesson about who he is and what he can do.

READ: MARK 4:35–41 (NLT)

As evening came, Jesus said to his disciples, "Let's cross to the other side of the lake." So they took Jesus in the boat and started out, leaving the crowds behind (although other boats followed). But soon a fierce storm came up. High waves were breaking into the boat, and it began to fill with water.

Jesus was sleeping at the back of the boat with his head on a cushion. The disciples woke him up, shouting, "Teacher, don't you care that we're going to drown?"

When Jesus woke up, he rebuked the wind and said to the waves, "Silence! Be still!" Suddenly the wind stopped, and there was a great calm. Then he asked them, "Why are you afraid? Do you still have no faith?"

The disciples were absolutely terrified. "Who is this man?" they asked each other. "Even the wind and waves obey him!"

TALK ABOUT IT
- How do you think the disciples felt when the storm started?
- Have you ever been scared around lots of water, or by a storm?

- Do you remember what the Israelites' reaction was to Moses when he brought them to the Red Sea? How is the disciples' reaction similar to the Israelites'?
- What would your reaction be if someone told the sea to be still and the storm to be silent, and the wind and waves obeyed?
- How do the disciples feel after Jesus calms the storm?
- Is it strange to think of Jesus (God) being asleep?
- Is there anything that confuses you about this story? If so, it's okay! Do you have any questions about Mark 4:35–41? It's time to ask your questions about the Bible.

CLOSING THOUGHT

The disciples would have known the stories of God we have been studying from the Old Testament. They would have remembered God separating the waters in the creation account. They would have known the story of Noah and the flood, the story of Moses and the Israelites crossing the sea. So when they saw Jesus, who had just taught them a bunch of new ideas about the kingdom of God, taming the waves and calming the storms, they recognized there was something really different about him. He was someone to be taken very seriously.

There were many people before Jesus and after Jesus who were good teachers. But Jesus shows his disciples (and us) that he is more than just a good teacher—he is Lord of the Universe, Lord of the storms. These and other miracles elevate him far above the teachers of the day and help his disciples and followers (and us!) trust Jesus as the Son of God. In this story Jesus proves himself trustworthy and ever-present, even when we are afraid and experience doubt.

PRAYER PROMPT

God's protection and faithfulness appear everywhere in the Bible! Let's remind ourselves of his protection and shelter by praying through Psalm 91 (NLT) below. Read it together as a family in unison or take turns reading:

Those who live in the shelter of the Most High
    will find rest in the shadow of the Almighty.
This I declare about the LORD:
He alone is my refuge, my place of safety;
    he is my God, and I trust him.
For he will rescue you from every trap
    and protect you from deadly disease.
He will cover you with his feathers.
    He will shelter you with his wings.
    His faithful promises are your armor and protection.
Do not be afraid of the terrors of the night,
    nor the arrow that flies in the day.
Do not dread the disease that stalks in darkness,
    nor the disaster that strikes at midday.
Though a thousand fall at your side,
    though ten thousand are dying around you,
    these evils will not touch you.
Just open your eyes,
    and see how the wicked are punished.

If you make the LORD your refuge,
    if you make the Most High your shelter,
no evil will conquer you;
    no plague will come near your home.
For he will order his angels
    to protect you wherever you go.
They will hold you up with their hands
    so you won't even hurt your foot on a stone.
You will trample upon lions and cobras;
    you will crush fierce lions and serpents under your feet!

The LORD says, "I will rescue those who love me.
    I will protect those who trust in my name.

When they call on me, I will answer;
  I will be with them in trouble.
  I will rescue and honor them.
I will reward them with a long life
  and give them my salvation."

ACTIVITY: RECREATE THE STORM

Act out today's Scripture verses by assigning roles. One family member should be the storm (Be creative! Use props to make lightning and thunder sounds.), another family member or two should be the disciples in the boat, and another family member should be Jesus. The scene is a short enough one that you can each take turns being each character in the story. Repeating the story a couple of times will help you experience and remember God's presence and protection in the storms of life.

Sea of Galilee

The sea Jesus and his disciples crossed is the Sea of Galilee, fed by the Jordan River. Many of Jesus's disciples were fishermen and familiar with the ways the sea behaved. It was known for fishing, trade, and sudden, violent storms. Much of Jesus's ministry and teaching occurs around the Sea of Galilee. Hundreds of years before Jesus, one of God's prophets, Isaiah, said, "There will be a time in the future when Galilee of the Gentiles, which lies along the road that runs between the Jordan and the sea, will be filled with glory" (Isaiah 9:1 NLT). The prophet continues with one of the most memorable passages of prophecy about the coming Messiah (vv. 2–7), which is fulfilled in Jesus, our Everlasting Father, Wonderful Counselor, Mighty God, Prince of Peace.

Manna from Heaven:
God Provides

SETTING UP THE STORY

The Israelites seem to have a case of short-term memory loss when it comes to God's faithfulness. After God divided the sea and the Israelites made it through to the other side, a long period of wandering began. During this time, the Israelites learned who they were as the people of God, which meant a *lot* of relying on the Lord.

READ: EXODUS 16:1–35 (MSG)

On the fifteenth day of the second month after they had left Egypt, the whole company of Israel moved on from Elim to the Wilderness of Sin which is between Elim and Sinai. The whole company of Israel complained against Moses and Aaron there in the wilderness. The Israelites said, "Why didn't GOD let us die in comfort in Egypt where we had lamb stew and all the bread we could eat? You've brought us out into this wilderness to starve us to death, the whole company of Israel!"

GOD said to Moses, "I'm going to rain bread down from the skies for you. The people will go out and gather each day's ration. I'm going to test them to see if they'll live according to my Teaching or not. On the sixth day, when they prepare what they have gathered, it will turn out to be twice as much as their daily ration."

Moses and Aaron told the People of Israel, "This evening you will know that it is GOD who brought you out of Egypt; and in the morning you will see the Glory of GOD. Yes, he's listened to your complaints against him. You haven't been complaining against us, you know, but against GOD."

Moses said, "Since it will be GOD who gives you meat for your meal in the evening and your fill of bread in the morning, it's GOD who will have listened to your complaints against him. Who are we in all this? You haven't been complaining to us—you've been complaining to GOD!"

Moses instructed Aaron: "Tell the whole company of Israel: 'Come near to GOD. He's heard your complaints.'"

When Aaron gave out the instructions to the whole company of Israel, they turned to face the wilderness. And there it was: the Glory of GOD visible in the Cloud.

GOD spoke to Moses, "I've listened to the complaints of the Israelites. Now tell them: 'At dusk you will eat meat and at dawn you'll eat your fill of bread; and you'll realize that I am God, *your* God.'"

That evening quail flew in and covered the camp and in the morning there was a layer of dew all over the camp. When the layer of dew had lifted, there on the wilderness ground was a fine flaky something, fine as frost on the ground. The Israelites took one look and said to one another, *man-hu* (What is it?). They had no idea what it was.

So Moses told them, "It's the bread GOD has given you to eat. And these are GOD's instructions: 'Gather enough for each person, about two quarts per person; gather enough for everyone in your tent.'"

The People of Israel went to work and started gathering, some more, some less, but when they measured out what they had gathered, those who gathered more had no extra and those who gathered less weren't short— each person had gathered as much as was needed.

Moses said to them, "Don't leave any of it until morning."

But they didn't listen to Moses. A few of the men kept back some of it until morning. It got wormy and smelled bad. And Moses lost his temper with them.

They gathered it every morning, each person according to need. Then the sun heated up and it melted. On the sixth day they gathered twice as much bread, about four quarts per person.

Then the leaders of the company came to Moses and reported.

Moses said, "This is what GOD was talking about: Tomorrow is a day of rest, a holy Sabbath to GOD. Whatever you plan to bake, bake today; and whatever you plan to boil, boil today. Then set aside the leftovers until morning." They set aside what was left until morning, as Moses had commanded. It didn't smell bad and there were no worms in it.

Moses said, "Now eat it; this is the day, a Sabbath for GOD. You won't find any of it on the ground today. Gather it every day for six days, but the seventh day is Sabbath; there won't be any of it on the ground."

On the seventh day, some of the people went out to gather anyway but they didn't find anything.

GOD said to Moses, "How long are you going to disobey my commands and not follow my instructions? Don't you see that GOD has given you the Sabbath? So on the sixth day he gives you bread for *two* days. So, each of you, stay home. Don't leave home on the seventh day."

So the people quit working on the seventh day.

The Israelites named it manna (What is it?). It looked like coriander seed, whitish. And it tasted like a cracker with honey.

Moses said, "This is GOD's command: 'Keep a two-quart jar of it, an omer, for future generations so they can see the bread that I fed you in the wilderness after I brought you out of Egypt.'"

Moses told Aaron, "Take a jar and fill it with two quarts of manna. Place it before GOD, keeping it safe for future generations."

Aaron did what GOD commanded Moses. He set it aside before The Testimony to preserve it.

The Israelites ate the manna for forty years until they arrived at the land where they would settle down. They ate manna until they reached the border into Canaan.

TALK ABOUT IT

- How many months passed between when the Israelites left Egypt and before they started to complain to Moses and Aaron?
- What kinds of things do you complain about? (Admit it, you complain sometimes!)
- How does God answer the Israelites' complaints?
- Do you have a "day of rest"? What do you do on your Sabbath?

- Is there anything that confuses you about this story? If so, it's okay! Do you have any questions about Exodus 16? It's time to ask your questions about the Bible.

CLOSING THOUGHT

It doesn't take us long to forget the challenges of the past. It only took a little over two months before the Israelites started reminiscing about the "good life" they had as slaves in Egypt. Instead of getting frustrated with the Israelites, again and again God hears them and provides for them— from providing them food in the morning and evening to a day of rest in the Sabbath. Day by day, the Israelites learn who it is they should rely on.

We're still learning the same lessons the Israelites learned in the wilderness—to rely on God and trust God for what we need, resting in his grace, mercy, and provision.

PRAYER PROMPT

In the New Testament and modeled in the story of the Israelites in the wilderness, we find encouragement to ask God for the things we need. Use Jesus's model prayer (called The Lord's Prayer) as a place to start, from Matthew 6:9–13 (MSG):

> Our Father in heaven,
> Reveal who you are.
> Set the world right;
> Do what's best—
>   as above, so below.
> Keep us alive with three square meals.
> Keep us forgiven with you and forgiving others.
> Keep us safe from ourselves and the Devil.
> You're in charge!
> You can do anything you want!
> You're ablaze in beauty!
>   Yes. Yes. Yes.

ACTIVITY: JAR OF MEMORIES (OR LIST OF MEMORIES)

The Israelites set up lots of ways to remember how God was faithful to them. In today's story, they stored up some of the manna to show future generations the way God had provided for them. Collect things or write notes to remind you of how God has provided for you and your family, and place them in a jar. Keep your jar of memories somewhere you can see it regularly to be reminded of how God has provided for you and your family.

Forty Years in the Wilderness

The number "40" often symbolizes a season of testing or preparation. Moses spent forty years in the desert before God called him to help the Israelites escape Egypt. The Israelites wander in the desert forty years before they are allowed to enter the Promised Land. The number forty will pop up again and again throughout your study of the Bible, so just like some of the other numbers we've learned about before, pay attention when this one comes up! It means God is preparing for something more.

The Enemy, God, and Job

SETTING UP THE STORY

The book of Job (pronounced "JOH-b") is a long story about how people try to make sense of suffering, looking for ways and reasons why bad things happen to good people. It's a question we still ask today. Job's story doesn't provide many answers, but like many of the other stories we've read in the Bible, it shows us how we can interact with God. Let's read the introduction to the book of Job and then learn more about the rest of the story.

READ: EXCERPTS FROM JOB 1–3 (NLT)

One day the members of the heavenly court came to present themselves before the LORD, and the Accuser, Satan, came with them. "Where have you come from?" the LORD asked Satan.

Satan answered the LORD, "I have been patrolling the earth, watching everything that's going on."

Then the LORD asked Satan, "Have you noticed my servant Job? He is the finest man in all the earth. He is blameless—a man of complete integrity. He fears God and stays away from evil."

Satan replied to the LORD, "Yes, but Job has good reason to fear God. You have always put a wall of protection around him and his home and his property. You have made him prosper in everything he does. Look how rich he is! But reach out and take away everything he has, and he will surely curse you to your face!"

"All right, you may test him," the LORD said to Satan. "Do whatever you want with everything he possesses, but don't harm him physically." So Satan left the LORD's presence.

One day when Job's sons and daughters were feasting at the oldest brother's house, a messenger arrived at Job's home with this news: "Your oxen were plowing, with the donkeys feeding beside them, when the Sabeans raided us. They stole all the animals and killed all the farmhands. I am the only one who escaped to tell you."

While he was still speaking, another messenger arrived with this news: "The fire of God has fallen from heaven and burned up your sheep and all the shepherds. I am the only one who escaped to tell you."

While he was still speaking, a third messenger arrived with this news: "Three bands of Chaldean raiders have stolen your camels and killed your servants. I am the only one who escaped to tell you."

While he was still speaking, another messenger arrived with this news: "Your sons and daughters were feasting in their oldest brother's home. Suddenly, a powerful wind swept in from the wilderness and hit the house on all sides. The house collapsed, and all your children are dead. I am the only one who escaped to tell you."

Job stood up and tore his robe in grief. Then he shaved his head and fell to the ground to worship. He said,

"I came naked from my mother's womb,
   and I will be naked when I leave.
The LORD gave me what I had,
   and the LORD has taken it away.
Praise the name of the LORD!"

In all of this, Job did not sin by blaming God. (Job 1:6–22)

When three of Job's friends heard of the tragedy he had suffered, they got together and traveled from their homes to comfort and console him. Their names were Eliphaz the Temanite, Bildad the Shuhite, and Zophar the Naamathite. When they saw Job from a distance, they scarcely recognized him. Wailing loudly, they tore their robes and threw dust into the air over their heads to show their grief. Then they sat on the ground with him for seven days and nights. No one said a word to Job, for they saw that his suffering was too great for words. (2:11–13)

[Job said,]
"Oh, why give light to those in misery,
and life to those who are bitter?
They long for death, and it won't come.
They search for death more eagerly than for hidden treasure.
They're filled with joy when they finally die,
and rejoice when they find the grave.
Why is life given to those with no future,
those God has surrounded with difficulties?
I cannot eat for sighing;
my groans pour out like water.
What I always feared has happened to me.
What I dreaded has come true.
I have no peace, no quietness.
I have no rest; only trouble comes." (Job 3:20–26)

TALK ABOUT IT

- Has anything ever happened to you that has left you wondering why bad things happen to good people?
- What kinds of explanations do people give when bad things happen?
- How did Job's friends first respond to the suffering Job experienced?
- In your life right now, are you like Job, feeling hurt or injured by someone or something, or like Job's friends, witnessing someone else's hurt?
- What comforts you when you are sad or hurt?
- What do you think about God having conversations with Satan? Why would he allow that?
- What do you imagine when you hear the phrase "the heavenly court"?
- Is there anything that confuses you about this story? If so, it's okay! Do you have any questions about the beginning of Job? It's time to ask your questions about the Bible.

CLOSING THOUGHT

The tale of Job goes on for forty-two chapters, so we're only getting a small taste of what happened. After Job said he'd be better off dead than dealing with all of this pain and suffering, his friends proceeded to argue with him, looking for reasons why all of this trouble had come. It was a mystery they couldn't solve.

And then God speaks, but he doesn't provide an answer that Job expects. Instead, God answers Job with more questions (see Job 38–41). God asks Job, "Where were you when I created the world?" God outlines example after example of his handiwork, his creation, his strength, and his might. He tells Job and his friends, look, you aren't God. You don't need to know the reasons why things happen the way they do. You only need to know that I am God, and that you can trust me because "everything under heaven is mine" (41:11 NLT).

PRAYER PROMPT

Whether you are like Job or Job's friends right now, God is here. If you are hurting without an answer for that hurt, pray that God would surround you with his presence through comforting friends and family members. If you see a friend or family member's suffering, pray that God would help you know what that friend needs to feel the love and presence of God. Thank God for the ways he gives and takes away, how he turns our pain into strength, character, and hope for something greater.

ACTIVITY: THE OPPOSITE GAME

Despite their good intentions, Job's friends end up saying things to him that are not true or helpful—the opposite of what Job really needed! Play the opposite game with your family. Whatever your parent tells you to do, what would be the opposite? Describe your dinner in opposites. Describe the weather in opposites. Try to clean up a room or play a game while speaking in opposites. You get the idea!

Satan, the Accuser

While the Scripture translation we read today calls the accuser at the start of the story "Satan," the character who approaches God to talk about Job is not who we typically think of as Satan. This character in the story is a member of God's divine council (as a "son of God"), serving as one who tests the policies of God. He doesn't act independently of God and isn't inherently evil.[6] As hard as it might be to believe, God permits Job's suffering to take place. But as a result of this suffering he reveals more about himself, and ultimately hears Job's cries for relief and brings healing to Job's life.

The Test

SETTING UP THE STORY

Moses and the Israelites spent forty years in the wilderness being tested and prepared before they were ready to enter the Promised Land. Job unknowingly participated in a test of his trust in God. Today, we're going to see how Jesus went through a similar test in the wilderness.

READ: MATTHEW 4:1–11 (MSG)

Next Jesus was taken into the wild by the Spirit for the Test. The Devil was ready to give it. Jesus prepared for the Test by fasting forty days and forty nights. That left him, of course, in a state of extreme hunger, which the Devil took advantage of in the first test: "Since you are God's Son, speak the word that will turn these stones into loaves of bread."

Jesus answered by quoting Deuteronomy: "It takes more than bread to stay alive. It takes a steady stream of words from God's mouth."

For the second test the Devil took him to the Holy City. He sat him on top of the Temple and said, "Since you are God's Son, jump." The Devil goaded him by quoting Psalm 91: "He has placed you in the care of angels. They will catch you so that you won't so much as stub your toe on a stone."

Jesus countered with another citation from Deuteronomy: "Don't you dare test the Lord your God."

For the third test, the Devil took him to the peak of a huge mountain. He gestured expansively, pointing out all the earth's kingdoms, how glorious they all were. Then he said, "They're yours—lock, stock, and barrel. Just go down on your knees and worship me, and they're yours."

Jesus' refusal was curt: "Beat it, Satan!" He backed his rebuke with a third quotation from Deuteronomy: "Worship the Lord your God, and only him. Serve him with absolute single-heartedness."

The Test was over. The Devil left. And in his place, angels! Angels came and took care of Jesus' needs.

TALK ABOUT IT

- When was Jesus tested—when he was strongest, or when he was weakest?
- What kinds of things did the Devil use to test Jesus?
- What did Jesus use to answer the Devil?
- What do you learn about Jesus from these verses?
- Is there anything that confuses you about this story? If so, it's okay! Do you have any questions about Matthew 4:1–11? It's time to ask your questions about the Bible.

CLOSING THOUGHT

When Jesus comes out of the wilderness after forty days and nights, he is prepared to face the Devil's test. The Devil's questions are filled with shortcuts and taunts. He says that, as the Son of God, Jesus should be able to make things happen to serve himself (turn stones to bread). He should be able to avoid the pain of this world (by throwing himself off a cliff and being rescued by angels). He should be able to take charge and rule over everyone (by worshipping the Devil instead of God).

But Jesus was fully human *and* fully God. Even though he could turn stones to bread, be saved by angels, or immediately rule over everyone, he isn't that kind of God. He doesn't take the easy way out. Instead, he is a God of freedom. He is a God of justice. He is a God of patience and mercy and service. The Devil tries to get Jesus to do things to meet Jesus's human needs and wants (food, safety, power), but Jesus says no way, I'm not that kind of God. I'm not here to serve my needs; I'm here to serve my Father and what it is he calls me to do.

PRAYER PROMPT

Thank God for his example in Jesus of how we can rely on God and on the direction of his Word to help us navigate tests and temptations. Pray that God will provide you with clarity and direction as you interact with others. Open your ears to what God is saying through the still, small voice that shows us the way and says to walk in it.

ACTIVITY: SHARE GOD'S BREAD WITH OTHERS

The Devil tempted Jesus with bread. After forty days in the wilderness, Jesus was likely starving for something good to eat. Choose a friend, neighbor, or maybe even a stranger to buy (or bake, if you've got the time or energy!) a loaf of bread this week. Make a card with all of the things you love about God and include it with your loaf of bread.

What's Deuteronomy?

All three of Jesus's responses to the Devil are quotes that come from the book of Deuteronomy. It is the fifth book in the Bible and is made up of three speeches delivered by Moses to the people of Israel. The first speech tells about the time the Israelites spent in the wilderness and then recounts the giving of the Ten Commandments, urging the people to follow the commandments and pass them on to their children. The second speech urges the people to follow the One True God rather than the multiple gods of the cultures that surrounded them, and to follow the law. The third speech tells the hopeful story that, even if the Israelites messed it all up, when they turned back to God, they would be restored. Our God is a god of restoration!

Ten Commandments

SETTING UP THE STORY

Last time we read about Jesus's test in the desert and how Jesus put God's Law at the center of how he lived. Today, we'll learn about that Law—the Ten Commandments—and see how the people responded. Remember how the Israelites were wandering in the desert for forty years, a number that means a time of preparation? God delivered the Ten Commandments to the Israelites when they were still wandering in the desert. By giving them these laws, he prepared them for everything ahead they would face.

READ: EXODUS 20:1–21 (NIV)

The number of each commandment is placed in parentheses after the commandment for referencing later.

And God spoke all these words:

"I am the Lord your God, who brought you out of Egypt, out of the land of slavery.

"You shall have no other gods before me. (1)

"You shall not make for yourself an image in the form of anything in heaven above or on the earth beneath or in the waters below. You shall not bow down to them or worship them; for I, the Lord your God, am a jealous God, punishing the children for the sin of the parents to the third and fourth generation of those who hate me, but showing love to a thousand generations of those who love me and keep my commandments. (2)

"You shall not misuse the name of the Lord your God, for the Lord will not hold anyone guiltless who misuses his name. (3)

"Remember the Sabbath day by keeping it holy. Six days you shall labor and do all your work, but the seventh day is a sabbath to the LORD your God. On it you shall not do any work, neither you, nor your son or daughter, nor your male or female servant, nor your animals, nor any foreigner residing in your towns. For in six days the LORD made the heavens and the earth, the sea, and all that is in them, but he rested on the seventh day. Therefore the LORD blessed the Sabbath day and made it holy. (4)

"Honor your father and your mother, so that you may live long in the land the LORD your God is giving you. (5)

"You shall not murder. (6)

"You shall not commit adultery. (7)

"You shall not steal. (8)

"You shall not give false testimony against your neighbor. (9)

"You shall not covet your neighbor's house. You shall not covet your neighbor's wife, or his male or female servant, his ox or donkey, or anything that belongs to your neighbor." (10)

When the people saw the thunder and lightning and heard the trumpet and saw the mountain in smoke, they trembled with fear. They stayed at a distance and said to Moses, "Speak to us yourself and we will listen. But do not have God speak to us or we will die."

Moses said to the people, "Do not be afraid. God has come to test you, so that the fear of God will be with you to keep you from sinning."

The people remained at a distance, while Moses approached the thick darkness where God was.

TALK ABOUT IT

- Read through each commandment one at a time again and discuss what they mean for you. How does God's Law apply to our family's life and our world today? There might be some words that need to be clarified, so don't be afraid to look them up or ask questions about what they mean.
- Is there anything that confuses you about this story? If so, it's okay! Do you have any questions about Exodus 20:1–21? It's time to ask your questions about the Bible.

CLOSING THOUGHT

The Ten Commandments stand the test of time. Ask any friend or stranger whether it is right to steal, to kill, to break vows (commit adultery), or to want someone else's stuff (covet), and they'll say of course those things are wrong. Should you honor your father and mother? Every culture everywhere calls this right and true. What about taking time to rest each week? This is super important to the rhythm of our bodies—when we don't take breaks, vacations, or days off during the week, everything in our system suffers, from our bodies to our minds to our emotions and spirits.

Jesus says that all of the laws (these ten commandments and the tons of codes and requirements written after) and all of the prophets (all of the teachings that make up a big portion of the Old Testament) are summed up in these two commandments: "Love the Lord your God with all your heart and with all your soul and with all your mind," and "Love your neighbor as yourself" (Matthew 22:37–39 NIV).

Can you see how the Ten Commandments fit into these two statements?

PRAYER PROMPT

The psalmist in Psalm 119 celebrated the Law, praising it for guidance and wisdom. The psalmist had a lot to say about God's Law in this psalm—it is 176 verses long! It might seem strange to celebrate rules, but as we've learned today, God's Law is his way of saying here is how you ought to love each other, and here is how you ought to love God. Let's pray together this excerpt from Psalm 119:97–104:

> Oh, how I love your law!
>   I meditate on it all day long.
> Your commands are always with me
>   and make me wiser than my enemies.
> I have more insight than all my teachers,
>   for I meditate on your statutes.
> I have more understanding than the elders,
>   for I obey your precepts.
> I have kept my feet from every evil path

so that I might obey your word.
I have not departed from your laws,
for you yourself have taught me.
How sweet are your words to my taste,
sweeter than honey to my mouth!
I gain understanding from your precepts;
therefore I hate every wrong path.

ACTIVITY: SUM IT UP

When the original Ten Commandments were written in Hebrew, they were summed up in one or two word phrases, just enough that they were easy to memorize and carry in your heart. See if you can simplify the Ten Commandments into super-short sentences (try to keep them under four words each). When you're done, post the list on your refrigerator or in your bedroom as a reminder.

Idol Worship

God says that he is a "jealous God, punishing the children for the sin of the parents to the third and fourth generation of those who hate me" (Exodus 20:4 NIV). Idols and other gods were being worshipped all over the place in the Israelites' time. People everywhere were trying to please their gods by sacrificing to them, making offerings to them, praying to them, and more. Whatever we put above God and his code (love him and love others) in our minds and in our daily lives is an idol. It can be anything we value more than God and people—money, sports, our country, fame, power, pleasure, food—you name it. If we put more value on it than we do on the people we're supposed to love and the God whom we serve, it's an idol.

The Beatitudes and the Salt of the Earth

SETTING UP THE STORY

The last story we read about Jesus was his test in the wilderness with the Devil. After that preparation, Jesus came out of the wilderness, gathered disciples, and began teaching. The book of Matthew leads us from the wilderness of preparation right into one of the most important sermons ever recorded—the Sermon on the Mount.

READ: MATTHEW 5:1–20 (NLT),
which is a portion of the Sermon on the Mount.

Family bonus points if you want to read the full sermon found in Matthew 5–7.

One day as he saw the crowds gathering, Jesus went up on the mountainside and sat down. His disciples gathered around him, and he began to teach them.

"God blesses those who are poor and realize their need for him,
> for the Kingdom of Heaven is theirs.
God blesses those who mourn,
> for they will be comforted.
God blesses those who are humble,
> for they will inherit the whole earth.
God blesses those who hunger and thirst for justice,
> for they will be satisfied.
God blesses those who are merciful,
> for they will be shown mercy.
God blesses those whose hearts are pure,

for they will see God.

God blesses those who work for peace,

for they will be called the children of God.

God blesses those who are persecuted for doing right,

for the Kingdom of Heaven is theirs.

"God blesses you when people mock you and persecute you and lie about you and say all sorts of evil things against you because you are my followers. Be happy about it! Be very glad! For a great reward awaits you in heaven. And remember, the ancient prophets were persecuted in the same way.

"You are the salt of the earth. But what good is salt if it has lost its flavor? Can you make it salty again? It will be thrown out and trampled underfoot as worthless.

"You are the light of the world—like a city on a hilltop that cannot be hidden. No one lights a lamp and then puts it under a basket. Instead, a lamp is placed on a stand, where it gives light to everyone in the house. In the same way, let your good deeds shine out for all to see, so that everyone will praise your heavenly Father.

"Don't misunderstand why I have come. I did not come to abolish the law of Moses or the writings of the prophets. No, I came to accomplish their purpose. I tell you the truth, until heaven and earth disappear, not even the smallest detail of God's law will disappear until its purpose is achieved. So if you ignore the least commandment and teach others to do the same, you will be called the least in the Kingdom of Heaven. But anyone who obeys God's laws and teaches them will be called great in the Kingdom of Heaven.

"But I warn you—unless your righteousness is better than the righteousness of the teachers of religious law and the Pharisees, you will never enter the Kingdom of Heaven!"

TALK ABOUT IT:

- When you think of being blessed, what comes to mind?
- How does Jesus define being blessed by God?

- What does salt do for food? What does it mean to be "the salt of the earth"?
- What does Jesus say about the Law that the Israelites had been following?
- Is there anything that confuses you about this story? If so, it's okay! Do you have any questions about Matthew 5:1–20 ? It's time to ask your questions about the Bible.

CLOSING THOUGHT

Rather than beginning this famous sermon with traditional Jewish teaching on the Laws of Moses, Jesus begins by redefining what it means to be a follower of God. Followers of God are the "salt of the earth," they mourn, they are meek, and they are persecuted. They are not like the proud and self-righteous, rule-worshipping, religious leaders of Jesus's day.

Throughout the Gospels, Jesus pushes against the priests and teachers of the Law who have made the rules of God so strict the people have no way to operate under them. He doesn't throw out the Law; he makes the focus about the heart, not the head. He says, okay, you want to earn God's favor? Here are the stakes: God is perfect. He has Big Love for all of his children over all of the earth. Love with that kind of love.

And then Jesus goes and loves with that kind of love, all the way to the cross, all the way to resurrection.

PRAYER PROMPT

Jesus tells his disciples in Matthew 11:28–30 (NIV): "Come to me, all you who are weary and burdened, and I will give you rest. Take my yoke upon you and learn from me, for I am gentle and humble in heart, and you will find rest for your souls. For my yoke is easy and my burden is light." Praise God that his overarching commandment is to love, and that love is what steers our hearts and saves our souls. Praise God that Jesus walked this earth and died on the cross to save us from ourselves, from the burden of sin, and to show us the way to love.

ACTIVITY #1: HOUSE RULES

Make a list of house rules for your family based off of the Beatitudes we read today in Matthew 5. Practice the Beatitudes at home and watch how God blesses your family.

ACTIVITY #2: PASS THE SALT, PLEASE

With your parents' permission, try and add a little bit of salt with each of your meals this week. Take a bite of food without salt. Then take another with some salt. What does the salt do to the flavor? With this in mind, think about what it means to be "the salt of the earth."

Sea of Galilee as Stage

How is it possible that crowds could gather around Jesus near a lake and be able to hear Jesus preach? The Sea of Galilee's landscape and geography makes it possible! Depending on how the wind is blowing and where you stand, it's possible to hear someone speaking even from seventy feet away. The slope of the hill where Jesus gave the Sermon on the Mount is shaped like a natural amphitheater. The bowl shape captures sound waves and naturally amplifies them.

Jesus and the Rich Young Man

SETTING UP THE STORY

We've been learning a lot about God's Law and the teachings of Jesus in the Sermon on the Mount. Jesus keeps raising the stakes for his followers. Today, we'll read about one interaction between Jesus and a young man who has been doing all the right things according to God's Law, and yet Jesus challenges him to go even further. Perhaps Jesus will challenge you and your family today as well.

READ: MARK 10:17–27 (MSG)

As he went out into the street, a man came running up, greeted him with great reverence, and asked, "Good Teacher, what must I do to get eternal life?"

Jesus said, "Why are you calling me good? No one is good, only God. You know the commandments: Don't murder, don't commit adultery, don't steal, don't lie, don't cheat, honor your father and mother."

He said, "Teacher, I have—from my youth—kept them all!"

Jesus looked him hard in the eye—and loved him! He said, "There's one thing left: Go sell whatever you own and give it to the poor. All your wealth will then be heavenly wealth. And come follow me."

The man's face clouded over. This was the last thing he expected to hear, and he walked off with a heavy heart. He was holding on tight to a lot of things, and not about to let go.

Looking at his disciples, Jesus said, "Do you have any idea how difficult it is for people who 'have it all' to enter God's kingdom?" The disciples couldn't believe what they were hearing, but Jesus kept on: "You can't imagine how difficult. I'd say it's easier for a camel to go through a needle's eye than for the rich to get into God's kingdom."

That set the disciples back on their heels. "Then who has any chance at all?" they asked.

Jesus was blunt: "No chance at all if you think you can pull it off by yourself. Every chance in the world if you let God do it."

TALK ABOUT IT

- What was Jesus challenging the young man to do in order to get eternal life?
- Why do you think Jesus says that it's hard for people who "have it all" to enter God's kingdom?
- Do you find it easy or hard to part with your stuff?
- What makes you want to hold on to things?
- How do you think the commandment to "love your neighbor as yourself" applies to wealth and "having it all"?
- The disciples are pretty flabbergasted by this teaching because it's impossible to meet this standard! How do you think God makes it possible?
- Does this mean we're supposed to give everything away? Should we buy anything?
- Is there anything that confuses you about this story? If so, it's okay! Do you have any questions about Mark 10:17–27? It's time to ask your questions about the Bible.

CLOSING THOUGHT

The disciples are amazed at this teaching. It just doesn't seem possible. In fact, they call it impossible. And Jesus says, you're right. This is impossible for you to do all on your own. But with God, all things are possible.

But how? As we've been reading the teachings of Jesus, the main message Jesus delivers is one of the heart. He's asking, what is it that you say and do? Is it motivated by love, or is it motivated by self-interest? God's way is love, not self-interest. So when Jesus sees that the rich young man has been seeking to follow God's way all this time, he loves him for it, but he also challenges him to go even further. Do all the right things, follow the law, *and* love your neighbor as yourself by using your wealth to help.

PRAYER PROMPT

As a family, pray about your stuff. Thank God for what he's given you. Ask him for guidance about what your family should do with money. Pray that God will help you follow Jesus, even with the stuff you own.

ACTIVITY: LISTEN AND GIVE

Ask God this week to tune your ears for opportunities to give something away to someone in need. Do you know someone who is moving for the first time and needs furniture? Maybe you have a table they could use or an extra couch. Listen and look for opportunities to be generous with what you have, and when the Holy Spirit nudges you, act!

Camel or Rope? The Art of Translation

The Bible was originally written in three ancient languages: Hebrew, Greek, and Aramaic. Bible translators study these languages, and then produce Bibles in the languages we speak today so that we can understand and relate to the stories that shape our faith.

There's some tricky footwork that goes into translating texts. The phrase "a camel through the eye of a needle" is a good example. Some scholars say the word *camel* in Greek and Aramaic is a word really close to the word *rope*, and a very specific type of rope—one that would have been braided and used to tie ships to a dock. This would make a lot of sense, because Jesus's disciples were a lot of fishermen, and they'd be really astounded by the impossibility of fitting a giant rope through the eye of a needle—maybe even more so than a camel through the eye of a needle!

If you think it shouldn't be so hard to figure out the difference between "camel" and "rope," think about our own language—you can *park* your car, and you can go to the *park*. You can *sink* in the sand or you can wash your hands in the *sink*. You can *row* your boat, and you can put your boats in a *row*. Tricky!

Be Strong and Courageous

SETTING UP THE STORY

Forty years before today's story, Moses sent a group of men to scout the land God had promised them. They spent forty days exploring the food, the ground, and the cities. When they returned, they told Moses that the land was great, but the people there were fierce. We'll be destroyed, they said (see Numbers 13:27–33). They lacked faith to enter the Promised Land, so instead of entering in, the Israelites wandered in the wilderness for forty years. Today's story begins with the current leader of Israel, Joshua, sending in just two spies to scout the land. God told Joshua to be "strong and courageous" and to take the Promised Land.

READ: JOSHUA 2 (NIV)

Then Joshua son of Nun secretly sent two spies from Shittim. "Go, look over the land," he said, "especially Jericho." So they went and entered the house of a prostitute named Rahab and stayed there.

The king of Jericho was told, "Look, some of the Israelites have come here tonight to spy out the land." So the king of Jericho sent this message to Rahab: "Bring out the men who came to you and entered your house, because they have come to spy out the whole land."

But the woman had taken the two men and hidden them. She said, "Yes, the men came to me, but I did not know where they had come from. At dusk, when it was time to close the city gate, they left. I don't know which way they went. Go after them quickly. You may catch up with them." (But she had taken them up to the roof and hidden them under the stalks of flax she had laid out on the roof.) So the men set out in pursuit of the spies on the road that leads to the fords of the Jordan, and as soon as the pursuers had gone out, the gate was shut.

Before the spies lay down for the night, she went up on the roof and said to them, "I know that the LORD has given you this land and that a great fear of you has fallen on us, so that all who live in this country are melting in fear because of you. We have heard how the LORD dried up the water of the Red Sea for you when you came out of Egypt, and what you did to Sihon and Og, the two kings of the Amorites east of the Jordan, whom you completely destroyed. When we heard of it, our hearts melted in fear and everyone's courage failed because of you, for the LORD your God is God in heaven above and on the earth below.

"Now then, please swear to me by the LORD that you will show kindness to my family, because I have shown kindness to you. Give me a sure sign that you will spare the lives of my father and mother, my brothers and sisters, and all who belong to them—and that you will save us from death."

"Our lives for your lives!" the men assured her. "If you don't tell what we are doing, we will treat you kindly and faithfully when the LORD gives us the land."

So she let them down by a rope through the window, for the house she lived in was part of the city wall. She said to them, "Go to the hills so the pursuers will not find you. Hide yourselves there three days until they return, and then go on your way."

Now the men had said to her, "This oath you made us swear will not be binding on us unless, when we enter the land, you have tied this scarlet cord in the window through which you let us down, and unless you have brought your father and mother, your brothers and all your family into your house. If any of them go outside your house into the street, their blood will be on their own heads; we will not be responsible. As for those who are in the house with you, their blood will be on our head if a hand is laid on them. But if you tell what we are doing, we will be released from the oath you made us swear."

"Agreed," she replied. "Let it be as you say."

So she sent them away, and they departed. And she tied the scarlet cord in the window.

When they left, they went into the hills and stayed there three days, until the pursuers had searched all along the road and returned without finding them. Then the two men started back. They went down out of the hills, forded the river and came to Joshua son of Nun and told him everything that had happened to them. They said to Joshua, "The LORD has surely given the whole land into our hands; all the people are melting in fear because of us."

TALK ABOUT IT

- What do the two spies learn from Rahab about the people of Jericho?
- Why do you think Rahab hid the spies?
- When have you needed to be strong and courageous? Was it difficult? Why was it hard?
- Have you ever done something you knew was right even though your friends thought you were wrong? Share a time in your life when you protected someone, like Rahab did for the spies.
- Is there anything that confuses you about this story? If so, it's okay! Do you have any questions about Joshua 2? It's time to ask your questions about the Bible.

CLOSING THOUGHT

The Israelites in today's story were raised in the desert, toughened up by suffering and endurance, and taught to rely on God day in and day out for everything—even their daily food and water supply.

Because the two spies had practiced trusting God every day for the last forty years, when big things happened that required even greater trust in God, they were prepared. Trusting God requires practice. Even when our circumstances don't seem fair, our God is fair. Even when bad things happen, our God is good. Even when the way seems uncertain, our God is the Way.

PRAYER PROMPT

Thank God for his promise in Joshua 1:9 that God will be with you wherever you go, and ask God for the courage and strength to overcome fears. Tell God you trust him and know that whatever happens, he will be with you.

ACTIVITY: I SPY AS SPIES!

Did you know there were spies in the Bible? Dress up as spies. Head outside (or in your house if it's cold) and find a hiding place. From this place, play "I Spy," and count how many unique items you can see. Imagine being one of Joshua's spies. It wasn't a game for them!

Rahab the Prostitute

It might seem surprising to find out that a prostitute is a main character in an important part of Israel's history! Rahab is counted as one of the most influential women of the Bible because of her protection over the two spies in Jericho and her faith. Rahab saw and heard what the God of Israel had done, and she believed that their God was god of all. Rahab—a Canaanite woman, an outsider, and a prostitute—trusted God and joined Israel. Rahab is honored as a woman of great faith. She's also recorded as the great-great-grandmother of King David and one of Jesus's ancestors! God can redeem any life and bring healing, wholeness, and love when we trust him.

Trusting God, Even on the Water

SETTING UP THE STORY

Last time we learned how God encouraged Joshua to be strong and coura-geous, because God promised to be with him wherever he went. It takes a lot of trust to hear that message and obey what God says, no matter what's ahead. That's what it means to have faith—trusting God because of who he says he is, not because of what's happening around us. Sometimes we have to trust God in spite of what's happening! Today's story shows us how God insists that we trust him.

READ: MATTHEW 14:22–36 (NLT)

Immediately after this, Jesus insisted that his disciples get back into the boat and cross to the other side of the lake, while he sent the people home. After sending them home, he went up into the hills by himself to pray. Night fell while he was there alone.

Meanwhile, the disciples were in trouble far away from land, for a strong wind had risen, and they were fighting heavy waves. About three o'clock in the morning Jesus came toward them, walking on the water. When the disciples saw him walking on the water, they were terrified. In their fear, they cried out, "It's a ghost!"

But Jesus spoke to them at once. "Don't be afraid," he said. "Take cour-age. I am here!"

Then Peter called to him, "Lord, if it's really you, tell me to come to you, walking on the water."

"Yes, come," Jesus said.

So Peter went over the side of the boat and walked on the water toward Jesus. But when he saw the strong wind and the waves, he was terrified and began to sink. "Save me, Lord!" he shouted.

Jesus immediately reached out and grabbed him. "You have so little faith," Jesus said. "Why did you doubt me?"

When they climbed back into the boat, the wind stopped. Then the disciples worshiped him. "You really are the Son of God!" they exclaimed.

After they had crossed the lake, they landed at Gennesaret. When the people recognized Jesus, the news of his arrival spread quickly throughout the whole area, and soon people were bringing all their sick to be healed. They begged him to let the sick touch at least the fringe of his robe, and all who touched him were healed.

TALK ABOUT IT

- Why do you think Jesus waited until there was a storm to appear to the disciples?
- If you saw a man walking on water in the middle of a storm, how would you react?
- What does Jesus ask Peter?
- Imagine what the other disciples on the boat may have been feeling and saying as Peter climbed out. What do you think they were thinking?
- What is your favorite part of today's reading? How does it help you to know Jesus better?
- Is there anything that confuses you about this story? If so, it's okay! How has God shown you that you can trust him? Do you have any questions about Matthew 14:22–36? It's time to ask your questions about the Bible.

CLOSING THOUGHT

It seems like Jesus set the disciples up for this lesson—he wanted them to *need* to rely on him in order to make it through. He set them up to witness a miracle. In the midst of the chaos of the storm, they weren't expecting Jesus. They weren't expecting him to walk on the water to their boat. Peter was daring enough to test whether Jesus was God by asking to be invited out onto the water, but then he turned his gaze away from Jesus back onto what was happening around him. Then and only then did he start to sink.

This story helps us understand many things about Jesus. He is a rescuer. He loves doubters. You can trust him. And he is the place to put your focus when you are facing a storm.

PRAYER PROMPT

Thank God for his faithfulness to you and your family, and pray that he will help you trust him more and more. If there's something you feel like you are being called to do, but you are feeling afraid or anxious about doing that thing, pray that God would give you courage, direction, and trust to walk with him out onto the waves.

ACTIVITY: WHAT MAKES SOMETHING SINK?

Jesus and Peter were able to walk on the water because Jesus performed a miracle. When God created the world, he also created natural laws that still govern our world. One of them is that items with less density float, and items with more density sink. Fill up your bathtub or kitchen sink and see which items float and which sink. Does a coin float or sink? How about a paper boat? A plastic toy? Think about seeing Jesus walking on the water—a true miracle!

Who Is Peter?

Peter, or Simon Peter, was one of Jesus's first disciples. Like all of the followers of Jesus throughout history, he committed all kinds of blunders and mistakes. And yet Jesus called him the *Rock* (Peter means "rock" in Greek) on which the whole church would be built. Jesus loved Peter, just like he loves us. Throughout the Gospels, Peter seems like he's always trying to say and do just the right thing, but he keeps on messing it up. When Jesus was arrested, Peter denied knowing Jesus three times, and when Jesus returned from death, Jesus still loved him. Jesus saw beyond Peter's fear and flighty attempts to earn Jesus's favor and called him the Rock anyway. All along Jesus just wanted Peter to trust God. After Jesus rose from the grave, Peter was humbled and finally understood Jesus's unconditional love and mercy. Peter ends up leading the church in Jerusalem and being known throughout history as the father of the Christian church.

Praying Big Prayers: Hannah and Samuel

SETTING UP THE STORY

When we left the Israelites they were just about to enter the Promised Land through Jericho. After Jericho, the Israelites fought hard to secure the land God had promised them. During that time, military leaders and judges rose up to lead the people through different trials, but soon the Israelites would ask God for an earthly king to rule over them instead of God himself. Today we'll read about the arrival of a prophet who will listen for the word of the Lord and show Israel the way to the king God has chosen for his people.

READ: 1 SAMUEL 1 (MSG)

There once was a man who lived in Ramathaim. He was descended from the old Zuph family in the Ephraim hills. His name was Elkanah. (He was connected with the Zuphs from Ephraim through his father Jeroham, his grandfather Elihu, and his great-grandfather Tohu.) He had two wives. The first was Hannah; the second was Peninnah. Peninnah had children; Hannah did not.

Every year this man went from his hometown up to Shiloh to worship and offer a sacrifice to God-of-the-Angel-Armies. Eli and his two sons, Hophni and Phinehas, served as the priests of God there. When Elkanah sacrificed, he passed helpings from the sacrificial meal around to his wife Peninnah and all her children, but he always gave an especially generous helping to Hannah because he loved her so much, and because God had not given her children. But her rival wife taunted her cruelly, rubbing it in and never letting her forget that God had not given her children. This went on year after year. Every time she went to the sanctuary of GOD she could expect to be taunted. Hannah was reduced to tears and had no appetite.

Her husband Elkanah said, "Oh, Hannah, why are you crying? Why aren't you eating? And why are you so upset? Am I not of more worth to you than ten sons?"

So Hannah ate. Then she pulled herself together, slipped away quietly, and entered the sanctuary. The priest Eli was on duty at the entrance to GOD's Temple in the customary seat. Crushed in soul, Hannah prayed to GOD and cried and cried—inconsolably. Then she made a vow:

Oh, GOD-of-the-Angel-Armies,

If you'll take a good, hard look at my pain,

If you'll quit neglecting me and go into action for me

By giving me a son,

I'll give him completely, unreservedly to you.

I'll set him apart for a life of holy discipline.

It so happened that as she continued in prayer before GOD, Eli was watching her closely. Hannah was praying in her heart, silently. Her lips moved, but no sound was heard. Eli jumped to the conclusion that she was drunk. He approached her and said, "You're drunk! How long do you plan to keep this up? Sober up, woman!"

Hannah said, "Oh no, sir—please! I'm a woman hard used. I haven't been drinking. Not a drop of wine or beer. The only thing I've been pouring out is my heart, pouring it out to GOD. Don't for a minute think I'm a bad woman. It's because I'm so desperately unhappy and in such pain that I've stayed here so long."

Eli answered her, "Go in peace. And may the GOD of Israel give you what you have asked of him."

"Think well of me—and pray for me!" she said, and went her way. Then she ate heartily, her face radiant.

Up before dawn, they worshiped GOD and returned home to Ramah. Elkanah slept with Hannah his wife, and GOD began making the necessary arrangements in response to what she had asked.

Before the year was out, Hannah had conceived and given birth to a son. She named him Samuel, explaining, "I asked GOD for him."

When Elkanah next took his family on their annual trip to Shiloh to worship GOD, offering sacrifices and keeping his vow, Hannah didn't go. She told her husband, "After the child is weaned, I'll bring him myself and present him before GOD—and that's where he'll stay, for good."

Elkanah said to his wife, "Do what you think is best. Stay home until you have weaned him. Yes! Let GOD complete what he has begun!"

So she did. She stayed home and nursed her son until she had weaned him. Then she took him up to Shiloh, bringing also the makings of a generous sacrificial meal—a prize bull, flour, and wine. The child was so young to be sent off!

They first butchered the bull, then brought the child to Eli. Hannah said, "Excuse me, sir. Would you believe that I'm the very woman who was standing before you at this very spot, praying to GOD? I prayed for this child, and GOD gave me what I asked for. And now I have dedicated him to GOD. He's dedicated to GOD for life."

Then and there, they worshiped GOD.

TALK ABOUT IT

- Have you ever wanted something so bad it hurt? What was it?
- How was that longing satisfied? Did it just go away, or did you get what you longed for?
- Do you think it's okay to ask God for things? What's okay to ask from God?
- We've been doing a lot of praying with these talks. What do you think it means to pray?
- Is there anything that confuses you about this story? If so, it's okay! Do you have any questions about 1 Samuel 1? It's time to ask your questions about the Bible.

CLOSING THOUGHT

Some people think only pastors or priests can talk to God, but Hannah and many others throughout the Bible show us that ordinary, everyday people can talk to God through prayer. Our prayers don't ever have to be perfect—in fact, most of the recorded prayers in the Bible aren't scripted, perfect, clean versions of what we think God would want to hear. Instead, they are angry, sad, hopeful, grieving, praising, wailing, dancing outpourings to the God Who Hears. Any of us can pray to God the way that Hannah does, begging him to stop ignoring her, bargaining with him to grant her the desires of her heart.

We can pray to God when we feel angry. We can pray to God when we feel scared. We can pray to God when we are joyful. We can pray to God when we are sad. We can pray to God when we don't know what else to do. There is no script for praying!

PRAYER PROMPT

Let's read together Hannah's song that is written to praise God for what he did in 1 Samuel 2:1–10 (MSG):

> I'm bursting with God-news!
>> I'm walking on air.
> I'm laughing at my rivals.
>> I'm dancing my salvation.
>
> Nothing and no one is holy like God,
>> no rock mountain like our God.
> Don't dare talk pretentiously—
>> not a word of boasting, ever!
> For God knows what's going on.
>> He takes the measure of everything that happens.
> The weapons of the strong are smashed to pieces,
>> while the weak are infused with fresh strength.
> The well-fed are out begging in the streets for crusts,
>> while the hungry are getting second helpings.
> The barren woman has a houseful of children,
>> while the mother of many is bereft.

God brings death and God brings life,
brings down to the grave and raises up.
God brings poverty and God brings wealth;
he lowers, he also lifts up.
He puts poor people on their feet again;
he rekindles burned-out lives with fresh hope,
Restoring dignity and respect to their lives—
a place in the sun!
For the very structures of earth are God's;
he has laid out his operations on a firm foundation.
He protectively cares for his faithful friends, step by step,
but leaves the wicked to stumble in the dark.
No one makes it in this life by sheer muscle!
God's enemies will be blasted out of the sky,
crashed in a heap and burned.
God will set things right all over the earth,
he'll give strength to his king,
he'll set his anointed on top of the world!

ACTIVITY #1: PRAY ALL THE TIME

You can pray all the time by looking for and seeing God throughout your day. Choose a time each day this week when you and your family can share about a moment when you prayed to God (outside of any structured prayer you might do as a family). What did you pray about? How does praying make you feel?

ACTIVITY #2: WRITE A HANNAH SONG

Write your own praise song to God like Hannah's prayer after Samuel is born. You can make it as long or as short as you want, and if you want to do it as a family, take turns writing a line at a time. To get started, try singing to the tune of one of your favorite songs.

God-of-the-Angel-Armies

The Message Bible translates one of the Hebrew names of God, "LORD of hosts," as "God-of-the-Angel-Armies" (1 Samuel 1:9–11 MSG). In other translations, this same name for God is translated "the LORD of Hosts" or "LORD Almighty." When we read about God's angels in the Bible, they are always overwhelming creatures that have to start every one of their conversations with, "Don't be afraid!" Can you imagine a whole army of these kinds of angels? They must be so powerful. But who is more powerful? The God-of-the-Angel-Armies! The Bible calls God by many names to show the different sides of who he is and the ways we can relate to him. When we need a way to talk about how powerful and strong God is, we can call him God Almighty, Lord of Hosts, or God-of-the-Angel-Armies.

An Unexpected King:
Samuel, Saul, and David

SETTING UP THE STORY

After battling for years, the Israelites finally possessed the land God promised them. The tribes had been led by judges, but after they entered the Promised Land, the Israelites looked around them at the other nations and decided they wanted a king instead. God used Samuel, the prophet and son of Hannah, to choose Saul as the first king of Israel, but things don't go so well with Saul. Today, we'll learn about God's choice for a new king, and wouldn't you know it, our God of surprises chooses someone no one would have expected.

READ: 1 SAMUEL 16 (NIV)

The LORD said to Samuel, "How long will you mourn for Saul, since I have rejected him as king over Israel? Fill your horn with oil and be on your way; I am sending you to Jesse of Bethlehem. I have chosen one of his sons to be king."

But Samuel said, "How can I go? If Saul hears about it, he will kill me."

The LORD said, "Take a heifer with you and say, 'I have come to sacrifice to the LORD.' Invite Jesse to the sacrifice, and I will show you what to do. You are to anoint for me the one I indicate."

Samuel did what the LORD said. When he arrived at Bethlehem, the elders of the town trembled when they met him. They asked, "Do you come in peace?"

Samuel replied, "Yes, in peace; I have come to sacrifice to the LORD. Consecrate yourselves and come to the sacrifice with me." Then he consecrated Jesse and his sons and invited them to the sacrifice.

When they arrived, Samuel saw Eliab and thought, "Surely the Lord's anointed stands here before the Lord."

But the Lord said to Samuel, "Do not consider his appearance or his height, for I have rejected him. The Lord does not look at the things people look at. People look at the outward appearance, but the Lord looks at the heart."

Then Jesse called Abinadab and had him pass in front of Samuel. But Samuel said, "The Lord has not chosen this one either." Jesse then had Shammah pass by, but Samuel said, "Nor has the Lord chosen this one." Jesse had seven of his sons pass before Samuel, but Samuel said to him, "The Lord has not chosen these." So he asked Jesse, "Are these all the sons you have?"

"There is still the youngest," Jesse answered. "He is tending the sheep."

Samuel said, "Send for him; we will not sit down until he arrives."

So he sent for him and had him brought in. He was glowing with health and had a fine appearance and handsome features.

Then the Lord said, "Rise and anoint him; this is the one."

So Samuel took the horn of oil and anointed him in the presence of his brothers, and from that day on the Spirit of the Lord came powerfully upon David. Samuel then went to Ramah.

Now the Spirit of the Lord had departed from Saul, and an evil spirit from the Lord tormented him.

Saul's attendants said to him, "See, an evil spirit from God is tormenting you. Let our lord command his servants here to search for someone who can play the lyre. He will play when the evil spirit from God comes on you, and you will feel better."

So Saul said to his attendants, "Find someone who plays well and bring him to me."

One of the servants answered, "I have seen a son of Jesse of Bethlehem who knows how to play the lyre. He is a brave man and a warrior. He speaks well and is a fine-looking man. And the Lord is with him."

Then Saul sent messengers to Jesse and said, "Send me your son David, who is with the sheep." So Jesse took a donkey loaded with bread, a skin of wine and a young goat and sent them with his son David to Saul.

David came to Saul and entered his service. Saul liked him very much, and David became one of his armor-bearers. Then Saul sent word to Jesse, saying, "Allow David to remain in my service, for I am pleased with him."

Whenever the spirit from God came on Saul, David would take up his lyre and play. Then relief would come to Saul; he would feel better, and the evil spirit would leave him.

TALK ABOUT IT
- Who is someone you consider a leader? What makes them a leader?
- Why do you think David wasn't even brought before Samuel by his father when Samuel first arrived?
- What drew Saul to David?
- What kinds of things soothe you when you are angry, upset, or afraid?
- What does this story make you think about God?
- Is there anything that confuses you about this story? If so, it's okay! Do you have any questions about 1 Samuel 16? It's time to ask your questions about the Bible.

CLOSING THOUGHT
Throughout history, people have looked to the firstborn of a family as the leader and heir of kingdoms. Even today the firstborn often takes on a leadership role in families.

But throughout the Bible we see God doing something other than what people expect. God often chooses someone unexpected—the younger son, the woman, the child, or the foreigner—to complete his work. In our reading today, God chose David, the youngest of seven brothers, as the future king of Israel. He faces a long road of struggle against Saul before he becomes king, but for now, Saul loves him and turns to him for comfort and strength.

This is God's way with us too. He uses unexpected people to do his work, whether they are old or young, tall or short, strong or weak, athletic or musically gifted. God looks past all the things we elevate as signs of strength and leadership and into the heart to see what we're *really* made of.

PRAYER PROMPT

God calls David a "man after his own heart." Let's pray that we would each be men, women, and children chasing after God's heart.

ACTIVITY: WHO DO YOU KNOW?

Parents, talk about a time when you misjudged someone based on appearances or assumptions you made. What happened when you got to know that person? Challenge each other this week to think of one person you don't know very well and try to get to know them. Eat lunch with that other person. Invite them to play. Talk to a neighbor you don't know very well. At the end of the week report back to each other about what you learned about that person.

The "Evil Spirit" from the Lord

The Bible passage we read today says that God's spirit left Saul and an evil spirit from the Lord tormented him in its place. Because we're human and have limited knowledge, we don't always understand the way God works—or how our own bodies work! The people of Israel did not have the advantages of modern medicine we have. They did not know much about how our heart, lungs, muscles, digestive system, brains and more all work together—and how they sometimes don't work quite the way they should.

In Jesus's day, people accused him of being demon possessed because he drove out demons, but the Lord says that if "Satan drives out Satan, how can his kingdom stand?" Jesus tells us in the Gospels that this "evil spirit" isn't sent from the Lord. And yet today many of us, Christians included, battle spiritual, mental, and emotional demons. The darkness we face can overwhelm, but we have the benefits of modern medicine, psychologists, support groups, and therapists who can come alongside people to find hope. Through the full body of Christ, empowered with knowledge, wisdom, truth, and love, God doesn't abandon us to our inner demons. He meets us in our brokenness and struggles to provide comfort and healing.

David and Goliath:
The Full Armor of God

SETTING UP THE STORY

Today's story is the beginning of David's rise to power in Israel. It's a long story but one filled with action. Let's jump right in!

READ: 1 SAMUEL 17 (NLT)

The Philistines now mustered their army for battle and camped between Socoh in Judah and Azekah at Ephes-dammim. Saul countered by gathering his Israelite troops near the valley of Elah. So the Philistines and Israelites faced each other on opposite hills, with the valley between them.

Then Goliath, a Philistine champion from Gath, came out of the Philistine ranks to face the forces of Israel. He was over nine feet tall! He wore a bronze helmet, and his bronze coat of mail weighed 125 pounds. He also wore bronze leg armor, and he carried a bronze javelin on his shoulder. The shaft of his spear was as heavy and thick as a weaver's beam, tipped with an iron spearhead that weighed 15 pounds. His armor bearer walked ahead of him carrying a shield.

Goliath stood and shouted a taunt across to the Israelites. "Why are you all coming out to fight?" he called. "I am the Philistine champion, but you are only the servants of Saul. Choose one man to come down here and fight me! If he kills me, then we will be your slaves. But if I kill him, you will be our slaves! I defy the armies of Israel today! Send me a man who will fight me!" When Saul and the Israelites heard this, they were terrified and deeply shaken.

Now David was the son of a man named Jesse, an Ephrathite from Bethlehem in the land of Judah. Jesse was an old man at that time, and he had eight sons. Jesse's three oldest sons—Eliab, Abinadab, and Shimea—

had already joined Saul's army to fight the Philistines. David was the youngest son. David's three oldest brothers stayed with Saul's army, but David went back and forth so he could help his father with the sheep in Bethlehem.

For forty days, every morning and evening, the Philistine champion strutted in front of the Israelite army.

One day Jesse said to David, "Take this basket of roasted grain and these ten loaves of bread, and carry them quickly to your brothers. And give these ten cuts of cheese to their captain. See how your brothers are getting along, and bring back a report on how they are doing." David's brothers were with Saul and the Israelite army at the valley of Elah, fighting against the Philistines.

So David left the sheep with another shepherd and set out early the next morning with the gifts, as Jesse had directed him. He arrived at the camp just as the Israelite army was leaving for the battlefield with shouts and battle cries. Soon the Israelite and Philistine forces stood facing each other, army against army. David left his things with the keeper of supplies and hurried out to the ranks to greet his brothers. As he was talking with them, Goliath, the Philistine champion from Gath, came out from the Philistine ranks. Then David heard him shout his usual taunt to the army of Israel.

As soon as the Israelite army saw him, they began to run away in fright. "Have you seen the giant?" the men asked. "He comes out each day to defy Israel. The king has offered a huge reward to anyone who kills him. He will give that man one of his daughters for a wife, and the man's entire family will be exempted from paying taxes!"

David asked the soldiers standing nearby, "What will a man get for killing this Philistine and ending his defiance of Israel? Who is this pagan Philistine anyway, that he is allowed to defy the armies of the living God?"

And these men gave David the same reply. They said, "Yes, that is the reward for killing him."

But when David's oldest brother, Eliab, heard David talking to the men, he was angry. "What are you doing around here anyway?" he demanded.

"What about those few sheep you're supposed to be taking care of? I know about your pride and deceit. You just want to see the battle!"

"What have I done now?" David replied. "I was only asking a question!" He walked over to some others and asked them the same thing and received the same answer. Then David's question was reported to King Saul, and the king sent for him.

"Don't worry about this Philistine," David told Saul. "I'll go fight him!"

"Don't be ridiculous!" Saul replied. "There's no way you can fight this Philistine and possibly win! You're only a boy, and he's been a man of war since his youth."

But David persisted. "I have been taking care of my father's sheep and goats," he said. "When a lion or a bear comes to steal a lamb from the flock, I go after it with a club and rescue the lamb from its mouth. If the animal turns on me, I catch it by the jaw and club it to death. I have done this to both lions and bears, and I'll do it to this pagan Philistine, too, for he has defied the armies of the living God! The LORD who rescued me from the claws of the lion and the bear will rescue me from this Philistine!"

Saul finally consented. "All right, go ahead," he said. "And may the LORD be with you!"

Then Saul gave David his own armor—a bronze helmet and a coat of mail. David put it on, strapped the sword over it, and took a step or two to see what it was like, for he had never worn such things before.

"I can't go in these," he protested to Saul. "I'm not used to them." So David took them off again. He picked up five smooth stones from a stream and put them into his shepherd's bag. Then, armed only with his shepherd's staff and sling, he started across the valley to fight the Philistine.

Goliath walked out toward David with his shield bearer ahead of him, sneering in contempt at this ruddy-faced boy. "Am I a dog," he roared at David, "that you come at me with a stick?" And he cursed David by the names of his gods. "Come over here, and I'll give your flesh to the birds and wild animals!" Goliath yelled.

David replied to the Philistine, "You come to me with sword, spear, and javelin, but I come to you in the name of the LORD of Heaven's Armies—the God of the armies of Israel, whom you have defied. Today the LORD will conquer you, and I will kill you and cut off your head. And then I will give the dead bodies of your men to the birds and wild animals, and the whole world will know that there is a God in Israel! And everyone assembled here will know that the LORD rescues his people, but not with sword and spear. This is the LORD's battle, and he will give you to us!"

As Goliath moved closer to attack, David quickly ran out to meet him. Reaching into his shepherd's bag and taking out a stone, he hurled it with his sling and hit the Philistine in the forehead. The stone sank in, and Goliath stumbled and fell face down on the ground.

So David triumphed over the Philistine with only a sling and a stone, for he had no sword. Then David ran over and pulled Goliath's sword from its sheath. David used it to kill him and cut off his head.

When the Philistines saw that their champion was dead, they turned and ran. Then the men of Israel and Judah gave a great shout of triumph and rushed after the Philistines, chasing them as far as Gath and the gates of Ekron. The bodies of the dead and wounded Philistines were strewn all along the road from Shaaraim, as far as Gath and Ekron. Then the Israelite army returned and plundered the deserted Philistine camp. (David took the Philistine's head to Jerusalem, but he stored the man's armor in his own tent.)

As Saul watched David go out to fight the Philistine, he asked Abner, the commander of his army, "Abner, whose son is this young man?"

"I really don't know," Abner declared.

"Well, find out who he is!" the king told him.

As soon as David returned from killing Goliath, Abner brought him to Saul with the Philistine's head still in his hand. "Tell me about your father, young man," Saul said.

And David replied, "His name is Jesse, and we live in Bethlehem."

TALK ABOUT IT
- Have you ever felt bullied by someone? How did it make you feel?
- Can you relate to the Israelites who faced Goliath?
- How was David able to overcome the fear the Israelites were experiencing so he could face Goliath?

- Do you think God gave David the victory over the Philistines?
- Did you know there was a beheading in the Bible? What do you think about this?
- Is there anything that confuses you about this story? If so, it's okay! Do you have any questions about 1 Samuel 17? It's time to ask your questions about the Bible.

CLOSING THOUGHT

David and Goliath is one of many stories in the Bible of battles between different groups where lots of men, women, and children are killed. It's kind of surprising to see God's message of hope, love, and peace in the same book where we find stories of violent wars and killing in the name of God. But that's part of the history of our world and the history of the Christian faith—people have killed in the name of God.

David was a great warrior and leader who came up with a way to defeat Goliath that no one else had thought of before, by using a sling and stone. But after Goliath fell, the Israelites participated in the same kind of warfare that tribes engaged in at that time—they used swords to kill the enemy in their path. They counted those deaths as victories for Israel and for Israel's God.

Jesus shows us a different way in the Gospels, a way of nonviolence, compassion, and peace. He reveals the heart of God that beats for a peaceable kingdom on earth. (Bonus points! Read Isaiah 11:1–11.)

PRAYER PROMPT

Sometimes it takes more courage and strength to be a peacemaker than it does to be a warrior. Let's pray for those who are at war all around the world right now. Pray for God's mercy and peace to rise up through the people of God to end all wars and bring about a peaceable kingdom on earth.

ACTIVITY #1: THE PEACEABLE KINGDOM

The prophet Isaiah describes the kingdom of God in Isaiah 11:6–8. Take a moment and read it together. An artist named Edward Hicks painted a picture of what "the peaceable kingdom" might look like. (Your parents can help you find it online.) Make your own peaceable kingdom picture: Gather together old magazines and make a collage of predators, prey, and people of all different ages and races together.

ACTIVITY #2: ANIMALS AND THE KINGDOM

With your parent's permission, search the internet for facts about the animals listed in Isaiah 11:6–8. What do those animals eat? How do they hunt their prey? How do they kill their prey? Then reread Isaiah 11:6–8. Now that you know how these animals hunt, kill, and eat, what do you think about Isaiah's description of God's kingdom?

Who were the Philistines?

The Bible identifies five cities occupied by the Philistines: Gaza, Ashdod, Ashkelon, Gath, and Ekron (Joshua 13:3). The Philistines worshipped Dagon, a god they believed controlled fertility and crops.[7] To praise this god, the Philistines often performed child sacrifices.[8] God did not want the Israelites to fall into the same abominable practice as the Philistines, so he forbade human sacrifice.

Who Is the Greatest in the Kingdom of Heaven?

SETTING UP THE STORY

Last time we read about David and Goliath and talked about the peaceable kingdom God desires—his kingdom of peace and love that will one day be restored and established on earth. In today's lesson, one of Jesus's disciples asks Jesus a question about the kingdom. Let's find out how Jesus answers.

READ: MATTHEW 18 (MSG)

At about the same time, the disciples came to Jesus asking, "Who gets the highest rank in God's kingdom?"

For an answer Jesus called over a child, whom he stood in the middle of the room, and said, "I'm telling you, once and for all, that unless you return to square one and start over like children, you're not even going to get a look at the kingdom, let alone get in. Whoever becomes simple and elemental again, like this child, will rank high in God's kingdom. What's more, when you receive the childlike on my account, it's the same as receiving me.

"But if you give them a hard time, bullying or taking advantage of their simple trust, you'll soon wish you hadn't. You'd be better off dropped in the middle of the lake with a millstone around your neck. Doom to the world for giving these God-believing children a hard time! Hard times are inevitable, but you don't have to make it worse—and it's doomsday to you if you do.

"If your hand or your foot gets in the way of God, chop it off and throw it away. You're better off maimed or lame and alive than the proud owners of two hands and two feet, godless in a furnace of eternal fire. And if your eye distracts you from God, pull it out and throw it away. You're better off one-eyed and alive than exercising your twenty-twenty vision from inside the fire of hell.

"Watch that you don't treat a single one of these childlike believers arrogantly. You realize, don't you, that their personal angels are constantly in touch with my Father in heaven?

"Look at it this way. If someone has a hundred sheep and one of them wanders off, doesn't he leave the ninety-nine and go after the one? And if he finds it, doesn't he make far more over it than over the ninety-nine who stay put? Your Father in heaven feels the same way. He doesn't want to lose even one of these simple believers.

"If a fellow believer hurts you, go and tell him—work it out between the two of you. If he listens, you've made a friend. If he won't listen, take one or two others along so that the presence of witnesses will keep things honest, and try again. If he still won't listen, tell the church. If he won't listen to the church, you'll have to start over from scratch, confront him with the need for repentance, and offer again God's forgiving love.

"Take this most seriously: A yes on earth is yes in heaven; a no on earth is no in heaven. What you say to one another is eternal. I mean this. When two of you get together on anything at all on earth and make a prayer of it, my Father in heaven goes into action. And when two or three of you are together because of me, you can be sure that I'll be there."

At that point Peter got up the nerve to ask, "Master, how many times do I forgive a brother or sister who hurts me? Seven?"

Jesus replied, "Seven! Hardly. Try seventy times seven.

"The kingdom of God is like a king who decided to square accounts with his servants. As he got underway, one servant was brought before him who had run up a debt of a hundred thousand dollars. He couldn't pay up, so the king ordered the man, along with his wife, children, and goods, to be auctioned off at the slave market.

"The poor wretch threw himself at the king's feet and begged, 'Give me a chance and I'll pay it all back.' Touched by his plea, the king let him off, erasing the debt.

"The servant was no sooner out of the room when he came upon one of his fellow servants who owed him ten dollars. He seized him by the throat and demanded, 'Pay up. Now!'

"The poor wretch threw himself down and begged, 'Give me a chance and I'll pay it all back.' But he wouldn't do it. He had him arrested and put in jail until the debt was paid. When the other servants saw this going on, they were outraged and brought a detailed report to the king.

"The king summoned the man and said, 'You evil servant! I forgave your entire debt when you begged me for mercy. Shouldn't you be compelled to be merciful to your fellow servant who asked for mercy?' The king was furious and put the screws to the man until he paid back his entire debt. And that's exactly what my Father in heaven is going to do to each one of you who doesn't forgive unconditionally anyone who asks for mercy."

TALK ABOUT IT

- Who does Jesus say is the greatest in the kingdom of heaven?
- Why do you think Jesus praises children as the greatest in the kingdom of heaven? What are some things that kids do different from adults?
- How does it make you feel to know that God will leave the ninety-nine and go looking for the one that wanders away?
- Has someone ever hurt your feelings? How have you dealt with that hurt?
- Do you find it easy or difficult to forgive?
- What does today's story make you think about God?
- Is there anything that confuses you about this story? If so, it's okay! Do you have any questions about Matthew 18? It's time to ask your questions about the Bible.

CLOSING THOUGHT

When the disciples ask who is the greatest in the kingdom, Jesus points to the child in the room because children are really good at love, trust, and hope. They are really good at making friends and really good at expressing their feelings when they get hurt.

These things matter a lot to Jesus, because people matter a lot to Jesus. They matter so much that he says there are big consequences for those who don't make a way for love. God's righteous anger and justice rises up on behalf of the weak, innocent, and oppressed. The king will hold those who are not merciful accountable. Jesus demonstrated to the world what real love, mercy, and forgiveness look like. As a Jesus follower, will you return to the world the same measure of love, mercy, and forgiveness that you've received?

It's a big calling, but it's worth all of eternity.

PRAYER PROMPT

Let's pray today that God's Holy Spirit would open our hearts and our minds to forgiveness. Let's pray that God would make a way through our pain, our hurt, and our anger and help us to forgive people seven times seventy times—and more.

ACTIVITY #1: PRACTICING FORGIVENESS

Forgiveness is hard work, but we can practice it daily. This week, when someone hurts your feelings, try this model for forgiveness: Tell someone what happened. Say how that made you feel. Forgive whoever hurt you. Renew the relationship or let go of the relationship. Practice this with your family and talk about the experience of forgiveness.[9]

ACTIVITY #2: HIDE AND SEEK

Play a game of hide and seek, remembering that Jesus doesn't quit seeking out the lost sheep until all one hundred of them are found!

How Children Were Viewed in Biblical Times

We learned earlier that the Philistines (and other ancient nations) practiced child sacrifice as a form of worship to their gods. By the time Jesus comes along, the attitude toward children wasn't much better. Ancient Romans viewed children as possessions. The father of a child could decide whether to keep a newborn or whether to abandon that child. Abandoned infants were assumed to be unwanted and could be picked up and raised as slaves.[10] The Hebrews have always considered children to be a great blessing from God, but they were still considered to be the father's possessions. The father could decide whether to sell his children into slavery and could even punish the child to the point of death. In order to make sure children grew into respectable adults, the Israelites made their education a high priority.[11]

David the King of Israel

SETTING UP THE STORY

Today, we'll learn more about David, the boy who became the king of Israel and was called "the man after God's own heart." After David killed Goliath, he gradually became the rock star of Israel. People everywhere celebrated his victories in battle. When we meet David today, he's already been king for ten years and is regarded as a powerful leader.

READ: 2 SAMUEL 11 (NIV)

*Bonus points for the family who reads the second half of the story in
2 Samuel 12:1–25!*

In the spring, at the time when kings go off to war, David sent Joab out with the king's men and the whole Israelite army. They destroyed the Ammonites and besieged Rabbah. But David remained in Jerusalem.

One evening David got up from his bed and walked around on the roof of the palace. From the roof he saw a woman bathing. The woman was very beautiful, and David sent someone to find out about her. The man said, "She is Bathsheba, the daughter of Eliam and the wife of Uriah the Hittite." Then David sent messengers to get her. She came to him, and he slept with her. (Now she was purifying herself from her monthly uncleanness.) Then she went back home. The woman conceived and sent word to David, saying, "I am pregnant."

So David sent this word to Joab: "Send me Uriah the Hittite." And Joab sent him to David. When Uriah came to him, David asked him how Joab was, how the soldiers were and how the war was going. Then David said to Uriah, "Go down to your house and wash your feet." So Uriah left the palace, and a gift from the king was sent after him. But Uriah slept at the entrance to the palace with all his master's servants and did not go down to his house.

David was told, "Uriah did not go home." So he asked Uriah, "Haven't you just come from a military campaign? Why didn't you go home?"

Uriah said to David, "The ark and Israel and Judah are staying in tents, and my commander Joab and my lord's men are camped in the open country. How could I go to my house to eat and drink and make love to my wife? As surely as you live, I will not do such a thing!"

Then David said to him, "Stay here one more day, and tomorrow I will send you back." So Uriah remained in Jerusalem that day and the next. At David's invitation, he ate and drank with him, and David made him drunk. But in the evening Uriah went out to sleep on his mat among his master's servants; he did not go home.

In the morning David wrote a letter to Joab and sent it with Uriah. In it he wrote, "Put Uriah out in front where the fighting is fiercest. Then withdraw from him so he will be struck down and die."

So while Joab had the city under siege, he put Uriah at a place where he knew the strongest defenders were. When the men of the city came out and fought against Joab, some of the men in David's army fell; moreover, Uriah the Hittite died.

Joab sent David a full account of the battle. He instructed the messenger: "When you have finished giving the king this account of the battle, the king's anger may flare up, and he may ask you, 'Why did you get so close to the city to fight? Didn't you know they would shoot arrows from the wall? Who killed Abimelek son of Jerub-Besheth? Didn't a woman drop an upper millstone on him from the wall, so that he died in Thebez? Why did you get so close to the wall?' If he asks you this, then say to him, 'Moreover, your servant Uriah the Hittite is dead.'"

The messenger set out, and when he arrived he told David everything Joab had sent him to say. The messenger said to David, "The men overpowered us and came out against us in the open, but we drove them back to the entrance of the city gate. Then the archers shot arrows at your servants from the wall, and some of the king's men died. Moreover, your servant Uriah the Hittite is dead."

David told the messenger, "Say this to Joab: 'Don't let this upset you; the sword devours one as well as another. Press the attack against the city and destroy it.' Say this to encourage Joab."

When Uriah's wife heard that her husband was dead, she mourned for him. After the time of mourning was over, David had her brought to his house, and she became his wife and bore him a son. But the thing David had done displeased the LORD.

TALK ABOUT IT

- How did David break God's commandment to love others? (Remember the Ten Commandments from Exodus 20?)
- God chose David to be the king of Israel. What did David do with this power in today's story?
- Do you think God forgave David for the wrong he did? Why or why not?
- Who were the people affected by David's decisions?
- Is there anything that confuses you about this story? If so, it's okay! Do you have any questions about 2 Samuel 11? It's time to ask your questions about the Bible.

CLOSING THOUGHT

David broke lots of the Ten Commandments in today's story: he desired another man's wife and brought her to the palace, he deceived Uriah, and he had Uriah killed. David used his position as king to take what wasn't his and sent men off to die at war to get his way.

It's hard to approach a friend when they are doing something wrong. Nathan, a prophet, put tough love into action. Nathan showed David what he did was wrong, and David was humbled and remorseful about his sins. And God forgave David (2 Samuel 12:1–25).

David shows us what it looks like to approach God when things in our life spin out of control. In David's crisis, he pleaded with God. He prayed. He fasted. David found the foundation of his purpose once more in trusting God.

You'd think this troubled start between David and Bathsheba would end in sadness, but Bathsheba had another son, and that other son was Solomon, who became the next king of Israel. God is there in the sadness, and God is there in the healing. We can trust him to be present with us in all things.

PRAYER PROMPT

David wrote Psalm 51 after the prophet Nathan confronted him about the sins he had committed (in 2 Samuel 12). Read Psalm 51 (NIV) together as a prayer we can say when we've done wrong:

> Have mercy on me, O God,
>   according to your unfailing love;
> according to your great compassion
>   blot out my transgressions.
> Wash away all my iniquity
>   and cleanse me from my sin.
>
> For I know my transgressions,
>   and my sin is always before me.
> Against you, you only, have I sinned
>   and done what is evil in your sight;
> so you are right in your verdict
>   and justified when you judge.
> Surely I was sinful at birth,
>   sinful from the time my mother conceived me.
> Yet you desired faithfulness even in the womb;
>   you taught me wisdom in that secret place.
>
> Cleanse me with hyssop, and I will be clean;
>   wash me, and I will be whiter than snow.
> Let me hear joy and gladness;

let the bones you have crushed rejoice.
Hide your face from my sins
>and blot out all my iniquity.

Create in me a pure heart, O God,
>and renew a steadfast spirit within me.
Do not cast me from your presence
>or take your Holy Spirit from me.
Restore to me the joy of your salvation
>and grant me a willing spirit, to sustain me.

Then I will teach transgressors your ways,
>so that sinners will turn back to you.
Deliver me from the guilt of bloodshed, O God,
>you who are God my Savior,
>and my tongue will sing of your righteousness.
Open my lips, Lord,
>and my mouth will declare your praise.
You do not delight in sacrifice, or I would bring it;
>you do not take pleasure in burnt offerings.
My sacrifice, O God, is a broken spirit;
>a broken and contrite heart
>you, God, will not despise.

May it please you to prosper Zion,
>to build up the walls of Jerusalem.
Then you will delight in the sacrifices of the righteous,
>in burnt offerings offered whole;
>then bulls will be offered on your altar.

ACTIVITY: I WAS WRONG—PRACTICING HUMILITY

When Nathan corrected David, David could have reacted in anger. He could have come to his own defense and sent Nathan away. Instead, David humbled himself and admitted his wrongs. He felt remorse for his actions.

Take turns making up silly things that you could be accused of doing wrong. What are the ways you could respond? Practice the wrong way and then practice the way David modeled in today's story.

Who was Uriah the Hittite?

Uriah was one of David's mighty men, the guys that stayed loyal to him while he was fleeing Saul. He probably fought side-by-side with David all those years. Uriah lived close enough to the palace for David to be able to see Bathsheba from his roof. Uriah stands in contrast to David in today's story as a man who was true to his word and loyal to his responsibilities.

The Woman Caught in the Act of Adultery: All Have Sinned and Fallen Short

SETTING UP THE STORY

The story we read last time began with an act of sexual sin committed by the King of Israel, David, "the man after God's own heart." "You shall not covet your neighbor's wife" is one of the Ten Commandments (Exodus 20:17 NIV). Another commandment is broken in today's story: "You shall not commit adultery" (Exodus 20:14 NIV). By the time of Jesus, the Israelites had established additional guidelines and punishments for breaking God's laws. But Jesus came with a bigger message. Let's read how Jesus answers the chief priests and leaders of his day.

READ: JOHN 8:1–11 (NLT)

Jesus returned to the Mount of Olives, but early the next morning he was back again at the Temple. A crowd soon gathered, and he sat down and taught them. As he was speaking, the teachers of religious law and the Pharisees brought a woman who had been caught in the act of adultery. They put her in front of the crowd.

"Teacher," they said to Jesus, "this woman was caught in the act of adultery. The law of Moses says to stone her. What do you say?"

They were trying to trap him into saying something they could use against him, but Jesus stooped down and wrote in the dust with his finger. They kept demanding an answer, so he stood up again and said, "All right, but let the one who has never sinned throw the first stone!" Then he stooped down again and wrote in the dust.

When the accusers heard this, they slipped away one by one, beginning with the oldest, until only Jesus was left in the middle of the crowd with the woman. Then Jesus stood up again and said to the woman, "Where are your accusers? Didn't even one of them condemn you?"

"No, Lord," she said.

And Jesus said, "Neither do I. Go and sin no more."

TALK ABOUT IT

- When you find out that your brother or sister or a friend has done something wrong, what do you usually do?
- How do you think the woman felt, standing in front of the crowd of people, in front of the religious leaders, and in front of Jesus?
- What were the religious leaders trying to accomplish by bringing the woman to Jesus?
- What message does Jesus give to the religious leaders? What message does he give to the woman?
- Is there anything that confuses you about this story? If so, it's okay! Do you have any questions about John 8:1–11? It's time to ask your questions about the Bible.

CLOSING THOUGHT

Every generation has its chief priests and teachers of the law who shame and punish people publicly for the wrong they do. The teachers and religious leaders want what is right and good and true, but in trying to follow the law, they miss the message of grace that Jesus brings.

Jesus doesn't just think about those on the *right* side of the law, he also cares for those on the *wrong* side of the law—those who have broken the rules, sinned, or made mistakes, like the woman in today's story.

Jesus knows we are all going to make mistakes. But in this story he shows us how to have mercy and leave justice to God. Jesus asked the woman, "Where are your accusers? Didn't even one of them condemn you?" and when the one who sinned answered no, Jesus said, "Neither do I. Go and sin no more." As a follower of Jesus, can you do the same?

PRAYER PROMPT

Pray that God will fill your family with his Holy Spirit so that we can remember he will bring about justice. Ask for his help to extend mercy and forgiveness, and to do whatever is in our power to bring peace. And when you sin and fall short of God's ways, pray for forgiveness and the strength to choose to "go and sin no more."

ACTIVITY: GIFTS FOR THE CONDEMNED

Find out what your community is doing to show mercy for those who are serving time for their crimes. Explore ways you can encourage prisoners—maybe write a note about God's love and mercy, and consider donating books through a books-to-prisoners program.[12] As Jesus modeled for us, perform an act of mercy for those who are facing the consequences of their actions.

What Did Jesus Write in the Dirt?

No one knows for sure what Jesus wrote in the dirt when he bent down, but it's possible that Jesus was demonstrating a verse that the teachers of the law would have been really familiar with, Jeremiah 17:13,[13] which was read every year at the conclusion of Yom Kippur (the Day of Atonement, a Jewish holiday): "LORD, you are the hope of Israel; all who forsake you will be put to shame. Those who turn away from you will be written in the dust because they have forsaken the LORD, the spring of living water" (NIV). All of the leaders standing around would have heard this verse every year of their adult lives, and the community right at that time was celebrating the Feast of Tabernacles and Yom Kippur (John 7:1–2).

When someone was caught in the act of adultery, they were supposed to bring both the man *and* the woman for judgment. The man wasn't brought along with the woman, so the priests themselves were breaking the Law. Maybe Jesus wrote these laws in the dust along with the names of the priests and teachers of the Law to emphasize how they were forsaking the Lord, "the spring of living water."

The Building of the Temple

SETTING UP THE STORY

We're going back into David's story near the end of his reign as king of Israel. After the incident with Bathsheba, all kinds of chaos and battles take place in David's family. There are silences and aggression, rape and murder, separation and reunions. Anything that could go wrong seems like it does go wrong for David and his family. And yet God proves again and again that it is his faithfulness, his mercy, and his love that endure through all things. He is the great redeemer of every story.

READ: 1 CHRONICLES 28:1–21 (MSG)

David called together all the leaders of Israel—tribal administrators, heads of various governmental operations, military commanders and captains, stewards in charge of the property and livestock belonging to the king and his sons—everyone who held responsible positions in the kingdom.

King David stood tall and spoke: "Listen to me, my people: I fully intended to build a permanent structure for the Chest of the Covenant of GOD, God's footstool. But when I got ready to build it, GOD said to me, 'You may not build a house to honor me—you've done too much fighting—killed too many people.' GOD chose me out of my family to be king over Israel forever. First he chose Judah as the lead tribe, then he narrowed it down to my family, and finally he picked me from my father's sons, pleased to make me the king over all Israel. And then from all my sons—and GOD gave me many!—he chose my son Solomon to sit on the throne of GOD's rule over Israel. He went on to say, 'Your son Solomon will build my house and my courts: I have chosen him to be my royal adopted son; and I will be to him a father. I will guarantee that his kingdom will last if he continues to be as strong-minded in doing what I command and carrying out my decisions as he is doing now.'

"And now, in this public place, all Israel looking on and God listening in, as GOD's people, obey and study every last one of the commandments of your GOD so that you can make the most of living in this good land and pass it on intact to your children, insuring a good future.

"And you, Solomon my son, get to know well your father's God; serve him with a whole heart and eager mind, for GOD examines every heart and sees through every motive. If you seek him, he'll make sure you find him, but if you abandon him, he'll leave you for good. Look sharp now! GOD has chosen *you* to build his holy house. Be brave, determined! And do it!"

Then David presented his son Solomon with the plans for The Temple complex: porch, storerooms, meeting rooms, and the place for atoning sacrifice. He turned over the plans for everything that God's Spirit had brought to his mind: the design of the courtyards, the arrangements of rooms, and the closets for storing all the holy things. He gave him his plan for organizing the Levites and priests in their work of leading and ordering worship in the house of God, and for caring for the liturgical furnishings. He provided exact specifications for how much gold and silver was needed for each article used in the services of worship: the gold and silver Lampstands and lamps, the gold tables for consecrated bread, the silver tables, the gold forks, the bowls and the jars, and the Incense Altar. And he gave him the plan for sculpting the cherubs with their wings outstretched over the Chest of the Covenant of GOD—the cherubim throne. "Here are the blueprints for the whole project as GOD gave me to understand it," David said.

David continued to address Solomon: "Take charge! Take heart! Don't be anxious or get discouraged. GOD, my God, is with you in this; he won't walk off and leave you in the lurch. He's at your side until every last detail is completed for conducting the worship of GOD. You have all the priests and Levites standing ready to pitch in, and skillful craftsmen and artisans of every kind ready to go to work. Both leaders and people are ready. Just say the word."

TALK ABOUT IT

- Why didn't God want David to build the temple?
- How do you think Solomon felt about his dad giving him these instructions and putting so much responsibility on him?
- When people encourage you, how does it make you feel?
- What do you think about the plan for the temple that David presented to Solomon?
- Is there anything that confuses you about this story? If so, it's okay! Do you have any questions about 1 Chronicles 28:1–21? It's time to ask your questions about the Bible.

CLOSING THOUGHT

Before the temple, the ark of the covenant (or "chest" in today's translation) was kept in a tabernacle, or tent. The ark of the covenant held some of the things that meant a lot to the Israelites and their religion. "This ark contained the gold jar of manna, Aaron's staff that had budded, and the stone tablets of the covenant" (Hebrews 9:4 NIV). The Israelites had carried the ark with them into the Promised Land.

To David, the tent didn't seem like the best place to put the ark of the covenant, so he decided he would build a house for the Lord. God didn't love this idea. He told David through the prophet Nathan that he had never lived in a house all the years he was with the Israelites, so why did he need one now? Instead, God provided his own plans to build a house for himself.

David's son, Solomon, built the temple for the Lord, and it was magnificent—all the best artists, craftsmen, materials, engineers, architects, and designers were called on throughout Israel to build the temple that David envisioned and that God directed.

PRAYER PROMPT:

Pray together that God's Holy Spirit would be loud in our hearts. Pray for the courage and strength to follow God, to trust God, and to be encouraged to follow God's ways in all things. Let's also thank God for his Holy Spirit and his ever-present love, mercy, and patience with us.

ACTIVITY #1: WORDS OF ENCOURAGEMENT

David's words to his son Solomon must have encouraged him greatly. Take turns speaking words of encouragement to each other. Go around the room and have each family member say something positive about one another. Take turns until each family member has said something encouraging to each person.

ACTIVITY #2: BUILDING INSTRUCTIONS

David passes on to Solomon very specific directions for how Solomon should build the temple. What do you think the temple of the Lord looked like? Draw, paint, build, or color a version of what you would build if you were making a house for the Lord. Use the creative gifts God has put in you to imagine what kind of temple you'd want to build for God, remembering that your body and life itself is a temple of the Holy Spirit. How can you build your life to be filled with God's presence?

Kings and Chronicles of Kings

There are multiple versions of the story of David and Solomon in the Bible. The first is in the books of Samuel and Kings. The second is in the books of Chronicles. The two stories are written over three hundred years apart! The books of Samuel and Kings are filled with drama, battles, and tragedies. The Israelites who wrote the earlier version wanted to show the consequences of having an earthly ruler in the kingdom instead of God as king. The books of Chronicles are much more focused on temple rituals. The second group of Israelites were living in captivity and missed the kings of old. They are two different accounts of the same stories, written to meet the needs of different readers, much like the four Gospels.

Jesus Clears the Temple

In today's story we meet Jesus in the temple courts. People came from all over the countryside to the temple in Jerusalem at Passover to offer sacrifices to God. Some people were selling animals to be sacrificed inside the temple courts. Let's find out what happens when Jesus comes into the temple right before Passover and sees all this happening.

READ: JOHN 2:13–22 (NIV)

When it was almost time for the Jewish Passover, Jesus went up to Jerusalem. In the temple courts he found people selling cattle, sheep and doves, and others sitting at tables exchanging money. So he made a whip out of cords, and drove all from the temple courts, both sheep and cattle; he scattered the coins of the money changers and overturned their tables. To those who sold doves he said, "Get these out of here! Stop turning my Father's house into a market!" His disciples remembered that it is written: "Zeal for your house will consume me."

The Jews then responded to him, "What sign can you show us to prove your authority to do all this?"

Jesus answered them, "Destroy this temple, and I will raise it again in three days."

They replied, "It has taken forty-six years to build this temple, and you are going to raise it in three days?" But the temple he had spoken of was his body. After he was raised from the dead, his disciples recalled what he had said. Then they believed the scripture and the words that Jesus had spoken.

TALK ABOUT IT

- Why was Jesus so angry at the people who were selling things in the temple courts?
- Why do you think this is such a big deal to Jesus? What does it matter if people sell stuff in the temple courts?
- What do you think the writer of this story means when he says "it is written"?
- If someone walked into your church and started flipping over tables, how would you react?
- Did you know that Jesus used a whip? Or that he got angry? What do you think about that?
- Is there anything that confuses you about this story? If so, it's okay! Do you have any questions about John 2:13–22? It's time to ask your questions about the Bible.

CLOSING THOUGHT

Hundreds of years before today's story, God spoke through the prophet Hosea, "For I desire mercy, not sacrifice, and acknowledgment of God rather than burnt offerings" (Hosea 6:6). But instead, the religious leaders aimed to make a profit off the people who were trying to keep the sacrificial rituals. They were trying to sell redemption.

But you can't buy redemption. Jesus tells the people in the temple courts, "destroy this temple and I will raise it again in three days." They didn't know what he meant, but we do—we know he meant his own body, which he sacrificed on the cross. He meant the end to the sacrificial system once and for all. *He* would be the Passover Lamb, sent to take away the sins of the world, so that everyone would have access to God's grace and mercy.

PRAYER PROMPT

Thank God for his ultimate sacrifice as the Passover Lamb and his ultimate resurrection. We don't have to practice the acts of sacrifice described in the temple. Pray for the ability to see and hear oppressed people, and for the courage and strength to do what we can in our power to seek justice and make a difference in our world.

ACTIVITY: BLESSING THE HOUSE OF WORSHIP

In today's story Jesus angrily cleaned out the Israelites' place of worship (the temple). Hopefully your place of worship isn't corrupt, but it still might need cleaning! Get together as a family and see if there is something unique that you can do for your church this week. Clean a room? Do some painting? Surprise the church staff with donuts? Figure out a way for your family to care for your place of worship, or its people, this week.

Sacrifice of Doves

Jesus specifically called out the guys selling doves in the text we read today. Why? The laws outlined by the religious leaders in Leviticus instructed that if you were too poor to bring a lamb as an offering, then you could bring two doves or pigeons instead. So the fact that people were trying to make a profit off of the sale of doves in the temple courts would have been even more offensive to Jesus. He's especially concerned about serving the poor, and when people were not just failing to help the poor, but taking advantage of them, you can imagine why he would have been upset!

Elijah and the Widow

SETTING UP THE STORY

After King David passed the throne to his son Solomon, the next guy to become king was Rehoboam. Under his rule, the kingdom of Israel split in two—into a northern kingdom (Israel) and a southern kingdom (Judah). A long history of kings ruled the two nations, battling other nations in the area. Sometimes the kings followed God and other times they did not.

Today's story is about Elijah, one of God's prophets, who lived under the reign of King Ahab, the ruler of Israel about two hundred years after David. Ahab did not lead the way God wanted him to. Elijah delivers some bad news to King Ahab at the beginning of today's story, and then Elijah is sent out, where he experiences God's mercy and provision in miraculous ways.

READ: 1 KINGS 16:29–33 AND 1 KINGS 17 (NLT)

Ahab son of Omri began to rule over Israel in the thirty-eighth year of King Asa's reign in Judah. He reigned in Samaria twenty-two years. But Ahab son of Omri did what was evil in the LORD's sight, even more than any of the kings before him. And as though it were not enough to follow the sinful example of Jeroboam, he married Jezebel, the daughter of King Ethbaal of the Sidonians, and he began to bow down in worship of Baal. First Ahab built a temple and an altar for Baal in Samaria. Then he set up an Asherah pole. He did more to provoke the anger of the LORD, the God of Israel, than any of the other kings of Israel before him. . . .

Now Elijah, who was from Tishbe in Gilead, told King Ahab, "As surely as the LORD, the God of Israel, lives—the God I serve—there will be no dew or rain during the next few years until I give the word!"

Then the LORD said to Elijah, "Go to the east and hide by Kerith

Brook, near where it enters the Jordan River. Drink from the brook and eat what the ravens bring you, for I have commanded them to bring you food."

So Elijah did as the LORD told him and camped beside Kerith Brook, east of the Jordan. The ravens brought him bread and meat each morning and evening, and he drank from the brook. But after a while the brook dried up, for there was no rainfall anywhere in the land.

Then the LORD said to Elijah, "Go and live in the village of Zarephath, near the city of Sidon. I have instructed a widow there to feed you."

So he went to Zarephath. As he arrived at the gates of the village, he saw a widow gathering sticks, and he asked her, "Would you please bring me a little water in a cup?" As she was going to get it, he called to her, "Bring me a bite of bread, too."

But she said, "I swear by the LORD your God that I don't have a single piece of bread in the house. And I have only a handful of flour left in the jar and a little cooking oil in the bottom of the jug. I was just gathering a few sticks to cook this last meal, and then my son and I will die."

But Elijah said to her, "Don't be afraid! Go ahead and do just what you've said, but make a little bread for me first. Then use what's left to prepare a meal for yourself and your son. For this is what the LORD, the God of Israel, says: There will always be flour and olive oil left in your containers until the time when the LORD sends rain and the crops grow again!"

So she did as Elijah said, and she and Elijah and her family continued to eat for many days. There was always enough flour and olive oil left in the containers, just as the LORD had promised through Elijah.

Some time later the woman's son became sick. He grew worse and worse, and finally he died. Then she said to Elijah, "O man of God, what have you done to me? Have you come here to point out my sins and kill my son?"

But Elijah replied, "Give me your son." And he took the child's body from her arms, carried him up the stairs to the room where he was staying, and laid the body on his bed. Then Elijah cried out to the LORD, "O LORD my God, why have you brought tragedy to this widow who has opened her home to me, causing her son to die?"

And he stretched himself out over the child three times and cried out to the LORD, "O LORD my God, please let this child's life return to him." The LORD heard Elijah's prayer, and the life of the child returned, and he revived! Then Elijah brought him down from the upper room and gave him to his mother. "Look!" he said. "Your son is alive!"

Then the woman told Elijah, "Now I know for sure that you are a man of God, and that the LORD truly speaks through you."

TALK ABOUT IT

- Why do you think God sent Elijah into hiding after he told Ahab about the drought?
- How does God provide for Elijah?
- How does God provide for the widow?
- Who is the ruler in your country?
- Where should we look for our provision, according to today's story?
- Is there anything that confuses you about this story? If so, it's okay! Do you have any questions about 1 Kings 16:29–33 and 1 Kings 17? It's time to ask your questions about the Bible.

CLOSING THOUGHT

Stories throughout 1 and 2 Kings show both good and bad leadership. Ahab is called one of the most evil kings in Israel. Elijah is one of God's prophets who stands up and speaks truth, even when his life is in danger. Sometimes the people who are in power abuse their power, make bad decisions, and cause the people they are leading to suffer.

As followers of Jesus Christ, we believe that God is the ultimate authority over nations. Whether ruled by good kings or bad kings, we are called to stand up for the weak and the oppressed. Through God, all these things are possible, and through God's people, we can be a light in dark times, if we walk with love and compassion for those who surround us.

PRAYER PROMPT

Elijah shows us how we can cry out to God and question what is happening around us. If you have questions about something that's happening in your world, ask God about it, and pray that he would give an answer. Pray for the leaders of your country to hear God and to rule as people who love God and love their neighbors.

ACTIVITY: PAY IT FORWARD

Talk about ways God has moved in your family's life, times when you've been unexpectedly blessed. What difference did it make for you? In today's story, the widow was able to trust God enough to be able to provide for Elijah, and Elijah was able to trust God enough to revive the widow's son. They each received God's provision through another person. Think about ways you can pay that gift forward. What can you and your family do this week to make a difference, through a random act of kindness or through an intentional gift to someone you know could use a blessing?

Zarephath

The city name of Zarephath comes from the Hebrew verb *sarap*, which means to "smelt, refine, or test."[14] The events that happen in Zarephath with the widow and Elijah certainly test them both. God shows us how seasons of struggle, pain, or challenge are used by him to refine us, just as Paul says in his letter to the Romans, "We can rejoice, too, when we run into problems and trials, for we know that they help us develop endurance. And endurance develops strength of character, and character strengthens our confident hope of salvation. And this hope will not lead to disappointment. For we know how dearly God loves us, because he has given us the Holy Spirit to fill our hearts with his love" (Romans 5:3–5 NLT).

Feeding the
Five Thousand

SETTING UP THE STORY

Last time we saw how God provided for Elijah and the widow during the drought. Today, Jesus will perform a similar miracle for the crowd who arrives to hear from him. Keep in mind what you learned about God and Elijah as you read today's story.

READ: MATTHEW 14:1–21 (MSG)

At about this time, Herod, the regional ruler, heard what was being said about Jesus. He said to his servants, "This has to be John the Baptizer come back from the dead. That's why he's able to work miracles!"

Herod had arrested John, put him in chains, and sent him to prison to placate Herodias, his brother Philip's wife. John had provoked Herod by naming his relationship with Herodias "adultery." Herod wanted to kill him, but he was afraid because so many people revered John as a prophet of God.

But at his birthday celebration, he got his chance. Herodias's daughter provided the entertainment, dancing for the guests. She swept Herod away. In his drunken enthusiasm, he promised her on oath anything she wanted. Already coached by her mother, she was ready: "Give me, served up on a platter, the head of John the Baptizer." That sobered the king up fast. Unwilling to lose face with his guests, he did it—ordered John's head cut off and presented to the girl on a platter. She in turn gave it to her mother. Later, John's disciples got the body, gave it a reverent burial, and reported to Jesus.

When Jesus got the news, he slipped away by boat to an out-of-the-way place by himself. But unsuccessfully—someone saw him and the word got around. Soon a lot of people from the nearby villages walked around the lake to where he was. When he saw them coming, he was overcome with pity and healed their sick.

Toward evening the disciples approached him. "We're out in the country and it's getting late. Dismiss the people so they can go to the villages and get some supper."

But Jesus said, "There is no need to dismiss them. You give them supper."

"All we have are five loaves of bread and two fish," they said.

Jesus said, "Bring them here." Then he had the people sit on the grass. He took the five loaves and two fish, lifted his face to heaven in prayer, blessed, broke, and gave the bread to the disciples. The disciples then gave the food to the congregation. They all ate their fill. They gathered twelve baskets of leftovers. About five thousand were fed.

TALK ABOUT IT

- Who is John the Baptist in relationship to Jesus? (Hint: we read about John the Baptist and Jesus in Luke 1.)
- How do you think the news about John affected Jesus?
- If you were Jesus when the people approached you, how would you have responded to them? Would you have wanted to help when you were feeling sad?
- Do you notice any parallels between today's story and the story we read last time about Elijah?
- Imagine being one of Jesus's disciples. What would you have thought when he said he would feed five thousand people with five loaves and two fish?
- Is there anything that confuses you about this story? If so, it's okay! Do you have any questions about Matthew 14:1–21? It's time to ask your questions about the Bible.

CLOSING THOUGHT

When Jesus found out about John the Baptist's cruel death, he retreated to be alone, but the crowds followed him. In the midst of Jesus's personal grief, he was still moved to perform miracles. He healed the people who came to him (like God healed the widow's son in the last story), and he fed the five thousand (like God provided food for Elijah, the widow, and her son).

This is how we overcome the tragedy in our world. When darkness attacks, we counterattack with light, with love, with food, with mercy, with hope. Jesus says elsewhere in the Gospels, "As long as it is day, we must do the works of him who sent me" (John 9:4 NIV). We must do the work. Jesus grieves the loss of John the Baptist, and then he refocuses, sees the world he is in, and does the work of God.

PRAYER PROMPT

Pray today for whatever crisis is currently happening in your world, whether personal, national, or global. Pray that God would reveal to you what it is he wants you to do. How can you respond in a way, big or small, local or far away, to spread love and peace in the world in the face of hate and pain?

ACTIVITY #1: NEIGHBORHOOD POTLUCK

Plan a potluck dinner, inviting people to bring dishes that remind them of a time that someone helped them through a difficult season. Share with your friends and neighbors your own dish's story.

ACTIVITY #2: SPREAD THE LOVE

Based on your prayer, share ideas you have for how you can be a part of God's love in action this week. Your ideas can be in direct response to the crisis you prayed about, or they can be something else entirely. What is your focus for love this week? Perhaps your church has a way you can put love in action this week.

More than Five Thousand!

The way women and children are viewed today is very different than how they were perceived throughout most of history. When the Gospel writers say there were five thousand in the crowd on the hill with Jesus, they wouldn't have been counting the women and children that were there too. This means that Jesus actually fed hundreds—maybe even thousands—more people with five loaves and two fish!

Elijah and the Prophets of Baal

SETTING UP THE STORY

After a three-year drought, God sent Elijah back to talk to Ahab. Ahab had been hunting for Elijah all that time, so this idea was very dangerous. Ahab's wife, Jezebel, was trying to kill all of God's prophets because she did not worship God—she worshipped the false god Baal. On Elijah's way back he ran into another prophet, Obadiah, Ahab's palace administrator. Obadiah couldn't believe that Elijah wanted him to tell Ahab he was back, because to do so could mean death for them both! But Elijah convinced Obadiah it was the thing to do. Let's find out what happened when Elijah confronted Ahab.

READ: 1 KINGS 18:16–46 (NIV)

So Obadiah went to meet Ahab and told him, and Ahab went to meet Elijah. When he saw Elijah, he said to him, "Is that you, you troubler of Israel?"

"I have not made trouble for Israel," Elijah replied. "But you and your father's family have. You have abandoned the LORD's commands and have followed the Baals. Now summon the people from all over Israel to meet me on Mount Carmel. And bring the four hundred and fifty prophets of Baal and the four hundred prophets of Asherah, who eat at Jezebel's table."

So Ahab sent word throughout all Israel and assembled the prophets on Mount Carmel. Elijah went before the people and said, "How long will you waver between two opinions? If the LORD is God, follow him; but if Baal is God, follow him."

But the people said nothing.

Then Elijah said to them, "I am the only one of the LORD's prophets left, but Baal has four hundred and fifty prophets. Get two bulls for us. Let Baal's prophets choose one for themselves, and let them cut it into pieces and put it on the wood but not set fire to it. I will prepare the other bull and put it on the wood but not set fire to it. Then you call on the name of your god, and I will call on the name of the LORD. The god who answers by fire—he is God."

Then all the people said, "What you say is good."

Elijah said to the prophets of Baal, "Choose one of the bulls and prepare it first, since there are so many of you. Call on the name of your god, but do not light the fire." So they took the bull given them and prepared it.

Then they called on the name of Baal from morning till noon. "Baal, answer us!" they shouted. But there was no response; no one answered. And they danced around the altar they had made.

At noon Elijah began to taunt them. "Shout louder!" he said. "Surely he is a god! Perhaps he is deep in thought, or busy, or traveling. Maybe he is sleeping and must be awakened." So they shouted louder and slashed themselves with swords and spears, as was their custom, until their blood flowed. Midday passed, and they continued their frantic prophesying until the time for the evening sacrifice. But there was no response, no one answered, no one paid attention.

Then Elijah said to all the people, "Come here to me." They came to him, and he repaired the altar of the LORD, which had been torn down. Elijah took twelve stones, one for each of the tribes descended from Jacob, to whom the word of the LORD had come, saying, "Your name shall be Israel." With the stones he built an altar in the name of the LORD, and he dug a trench around it large enough to hold two seahs of seed. He arranged the wood, cut the bull into pieces and laid it on the wood. Then he said to them, "Fill four large jars with water and pour it on the offering and on the wood."

"Do it again," he said, and they did it again.

"Do it a third time," he ordered, and they did it the third time. The water ran down around the altar and even filled the trench.

At the time of sacrifice, the prophet Elijah stepped forward and prayed: "LORD, the God of Abraham, Isaac and Israel, let it be known today that you are God in Israel and that I am your servant and have done all these things at your command. Answer me, LORD, answer me, so these people will know that you, LORD, are God, and that you are turning their hearts back again."

Then the fire of the LORD fell and burned up the sacrifice, the wood, the stones and the soil, and also licked up the water in the trench.

When all the people saw this, they fell prostrate and cried, "The LORD—he is God! The LORD—he is God!"

Then Elijah commanded them, "Seize the prophets of Baal. Don't let anyone get away!" They seized them, and Elijah had them brought down to the Kishon Valley and slaughtered there.

And Elijah said to Ahab, "Go, eat and drink, for there is the sound of a heavy rain." So Ahab went off to eat and drink, but Elijah climbed to the top of Carmel, bent down to the ground and put his face between his knees.

"Go and look toward the sea," he told his servant. And he went up and looked.

"There is nothing there," he said.

Seven times Elijah said, "Go back."

The seventh time the servant reported, "A cloud as small as a man's hand is rising from the sea."

So Elijah said, "Go and tell Ahab, 'Hitch up your chariot and go down before the rain stops you.'"

Meanwhile, the sky grew black with clouds, the wind rose, a heavy rain started falling and Ahab rode off to Jezreel. The power of the LORD came on Elijah and, tucking his cloak into his belt, he ran ahead of Ahab all the way to Jezreel.

TALK ABOUT IT

- How would you describe Elijah's actions in today's story?
- What did the prophets of Baal do to try to get their god to show up?
- What is the difference between the way the prophets of Baal worshipped their god and how Elijah worshipped God?

- When have you felt God's presence most? If you aren't sure what that feels like, think about a time when you have felt safe, at peace, or loved.
- Is there anything that confuses you about this story? If so, it's okay! Do you have any questions about 1 Kings 18:16–46? It's time to ask your questions about the Bible.

CLOSING THOUGHT

Elijah stood up to the foreign gods, helped demonstrate God's power, and came out victorious! The actions of Elijah and the actions of the prophets of Baal are worth noticing. Elijah prayed, waited, and trusted God. The prophets of Baal yelled, cut themselves, and begged for Baal to send fire. Elijah waited, confident that God would provide for him.

Disciples of Jesus can wait on God in confidence too. The same God who miraculously burned up Elijah's soaking-wet altar is the God to whom you can pray and trust.

PRAYER PROMPT

Pray to God today, confident that he hears you and that you can trust him. As a family, say this verse from Psalm 13:5 (NIV): "But I trust in your unfailing love; my heart rejoices in your salvation."

ACTIVITY: LITTLE ALTARS

Elijah built an altar to God using twelve stones to symbolize the twelve tribes of Israel. An altar is a space made to dedicate something—such as your family, your resources, your life, or a whole nation—to God. In churches, it's where tithes and offerings are placed. Build an altar of stones (or other materials) to God at the entrance of your home to remember your family's dedication to him. Have each family member choose a rock (or other item) to symbolize themselves and remember their dedication to God.

Baal

The name "Baal" was used often to distinguish other gods from the God of Israel. It was most often used in reference to the storm and fertility god Hadad. In today's story, God shows Elijah who he is *not*—he is *not* the god of the storm that the Baal prophets worshipped. He is a god of incredible power, enough to consume a dripping-wet altar. He is the One True God.

Jesus Heals on the Sabbath and the Pharisees Don't Like It

SETTING UP THE STORY

In our last story, we saw how Elijah stood up to a corrupt king and how God demonstrated his power and might. In today's story, Jesus will stand up for what's right, even though the people in power disagree with the way he does things. Let's discover how Jesus changes the way we are to view God's laws and the rules of religion. One important thing to know is that the Pharisees and teachers of the law had defined what it meant to rest on the Sabbath (the seventh day of the week, like our Sunday), and they had very, very strict rules about it.

READ: MATTHEW 12:1–37 (NLT)

At about that time Jesus was walking through some grainfields on the Sabbath. His disciples were hungry, so they began breaking off some heads of grain and eating them. But some Pharisees saw them do it and protested, "Look, your disciples are breaking the law by harvesting grain on the Sabbath."

Jesus said to them, "Haven't you read in the Scriptures what David did when he and his companions were hungry? He went into the house of God, and he and his companions broke the law by eating the sacred loaves of bread that only the priests are allowed to eat. And haven't you read in the law of Moses that the priests on duty in the Temple may work on the Sabbath? I tell you, there is one here who is even greater than the Temple! But you would not have condemned my innocent disciples if you knew the meaning of this Scripture: 'I want you to show mercy, not offer sacrifices.' For the Son of Man is Lord, even over the Sabbath!"

Then Jesus went over to their synagogue, where he noticed a man with a deformed hand. The Pharisees asked Jesus, "Does the law permit a person to work by healing on the Sabbath?" (They were hoping he would say yes, so they could bring charges against him.)

And he answered, "If you had a sheep that fell into a well on the Sabbath, wouldn't you work to pull it out? Of course you would. And how much more valuable is a person than a sheep! Yes, the law permits a person to do good on the Sabbath."

Then he said to the man, "Hold out your hand." So the man held out his hand, and it was restored, just like the other one! Then the Pharisees called a meeting to plot how to kill Jesus.

But Jesus knew what they were planning. So he left that area, and many people followed him. He healed all the sick among them, but he warned them not to reveal who he was. This fulfilled the prophecy of Isaiah concerning him:

"Look at my Servant, whom I have chosen.
   He is my Beloved, who pleases me.
I will put my Spirit upon him,
   and he will proclaim justice to the nations.
He will not fight or shout
   or raise his voice in public.
He will not crush the weakest reed
   or put out a flickering candle.
   Finally he will cause justice to be victorious.
And his name will be the hope
   of all the world."

Then a demon-possessed man, who was blind and couldn't speak, was brought to Jesus. He healed the man so that he could both speak and see. The crowd was amazed and asked, "Could it be that Jesus is the Son of David, the Messiah?"

But when the Pharisees heard about the miracle, they said, "No wonder he can cast out demons. He gets his power from Satan, the prince of demons."

Jesus knew their thoughts and replied, "Any kingdom divided by civil war is doomed. A town or family splintered by feuding will fall apart. And if Satan is casting out Satan, he is divided and fighting against himself. His own kingdom will not survive. And if I am empowered by Satan, what about your own exorcists? They cast out demons, too, so they will condemn you for what you have said. But if I am casting out demons by the Spirit of God, then the Kingdom of God has arrived among you. For who is powerful enough to enter the house of a strong man and plunder his goods? Only someone even stronger—someone who could tie him up and then plunder his house.

"Anyone who isn't with me opposes me, and anyone who isn't working with me is actually working against me.

"So I tell you, every sin and blasphemy can be forgiven—except blasphemy against the Holy Spirit, which will never be forgiven. Anyone who speaks against the Son of Man can be forgiven, but anyone who speaks against the Holy Spirit will never be forgiven, either in this world or in the world to come.

"A tree is identified by its fruit. If a tree is good, its fruit will be good. If a tree is bad, its fruit will be bad. You brood of snakes! How could evil men like you speak what is good and right? For whatever is in your heart determines what you say. A good person produces good things from the treasury of a good heart, and an evil person produces evil things from the treasury of an evil heart. And I tell you this, you must give an account on judgment day for every idle word you speak. The words you say will either acquit you or condemn you."

TALK ABOUT IT

- What was Jesus doing on the Sabbath that made the Pharisees so angry?
- Why do you think Jesus wasn't interested in following the rules the Pharisees defined?
- Can you believe that Jesus was accused by the religious leaders of being "from Satan"?
- How does Jesus respond to the accusation that he must be "from Satan"?
- What do you think Jesus meant about the tree and the fruit?

- Is there anything that confuses you about this story? If so, it's okay! Do you have any questions about Matthew 12:1–37? It's time to ask your questions about the Bible.

CLOSING THOUGHT

For years the Pharisees had been making sure they closely followed the rules in order to stay in good relationship with God.

But while the Pharisees were trying to keep a list of rules, Jesus was healing people, feeding people, and loving people. And that made the Pharisees really angry.

Jesus reminded them that following God isn't about rules; it's about loving God and loving people. Eventually, the religious leaders killed him for going against their rules, but because Jesus is the Son of God, not even their punishment could conquer God's love and grace! Jesus rose from the dead to show that he is Lord over everything and that love wins!

When we find ourselves getting overly wrapped up in the way we do things instead of *who* we do things for, we need to remember what Jesus said about the tree and the fruit—how we love others will show itself through our actions.

PRAYER PROMPT

Pray that God would show us any rules in our practice of Christianity that might actually take away from our ability to love others. Ask God for the humility we need to have our hearts moved and our actions changed. Thank God for the ways he continues to work in our lives, changing us, shaping us, and helping us to become the most whole and complete versions of ourselves, so we can love others well.

ACTIVITY #1: BREAK THE RULES FOR JESUS!

In most Christian circles, Sunday is church day. We treat it as our Sabbath. Sometimes we get into the habit of defining our relationship with God with the number of times we attend church. Our habit can become about following the rules instead of loving God and loving others. Talk with your family about why you go to church. What can you do this Sunday to make your church attendance about more than just going to church? If you're feeling *really* bold, skip church and do something to serve the orphans and widows in your community instead!

ACTIVITY #2: FAMILY GAME NIGHT

Families need to practice Sabbath—rest and relaxation—together. Plan a family game night. Focus on having fun and building each other up through encouraging words. Enjoy a break from school, work, and other stressors *together*.

"It Is Written . . ." Prophecies Fulfilled

The book of Matthew was written to the Jewish believers. The Jews had been waiting for the Messiah (the Savior) to come. For centuries the prophets had been warning the people of Israel to change their ways, as well as promising the arrival of a Savior. Matthew's Gospel makes reference to a lot of these prophecies to prove to the Jews that Jesus is indeed the Messiah they have been waiting for! Today's story made reference to two important prophecies—one we've read before from Hosea 6:6 ("I desire mercy, not sacrifice") and one long passage from Isaiah. These verses bring the Old Testament understanding of God into focus as Jesus revealed himself as the promised Messiah.

God of Many Chances

SETTING UP THE STORY

Last time we read about how Jesus and the Pharisees disagreed about rules and relationships. Today, we're going to read an Old Testament story about another person that had strong opinions about rules and relationships—Jonah. God shows Jonah what kind of God he is.

READ: EXCERPTS FROM JONAH 1–4 (MSG)

One day long ago, GOD's Word came to Jonah, Amittai's son: "Up on your feet and on your way to the big city of Nineveh! Preach to them. They're in a bad way and I can't ignore it any longer."

But Jonah got up and went the other direction to Tarshish, running away from GOD. He went down to the port of Joppa and found a ship headed for Tarshish. He paid the fare and went on board, joining those going to Tarshish—as far away from GOD as he could get.

But GOD sent a huge storm at sea, the waves towering. (Jonah 1:1–4)

Jonah said, "Throw me overboard, into the sea. Then the storm will stop. It's all my fault. I'm the cause of the storm. Get rid of me and you'll get rid of the storm."

But no. The men tried rowing back to shore. They made no headway. The storm only got worse and worse, wild and raging.

Then they prayed to GOD, "O GOD! Don't let us drown because of this man's life, and don't blame us for his death. You are GOD. Do what you think is best."

They took Jonah and threw him overboard. Immediately the sea was quieted down.

The sailors were impressed, no longer terrified by the sea, but in awe of GOD. They worshiped GOD, offered a sacrifice, and made vows.

199

Then God assigned a huge fish to swallow Jonah. Jonah was in the fish's belly three days and nights.

Then Jonah prayed to his God from the belly of the fish.

He prayed:

"In trouble, deep trouble, I prayed to God.
> He answered me.

From the belly of the grave I cried, 'Help!'
> You heard my cry . . .

Those who worship hollow gods, god-frauds,
> walk away from their only true love.

But I'm worshiping you, God,
> calling out in thanksgiving!

And I'll do what I promised I'd do!
> Salvation belongs to God!"

Then God spoke to the fish, and it vomited up Jonah on the seashore. (1:12–2:3, 8–10)

Next, God spoke to Jonah a second time: "Up on your feet and on your way to the big city of Nineveh! Preach to them. They're in a bad way and I can't ignore it any longer."

This time Jonah started off straight for Nineveh, obeying God's orders to the letter.

Nineveh was a big city, very big—it took three days to walk across it.

Jonah entered the city, went one day's walk and preached, "In forty days Nineveh will be smashed."

The people of Nineveh listened, and trusted God. They proclaimed a citywide fast and dressed in burlap to show their repentance. Everyone did it—rich and poor, famous and obscure, leaders and followers. (3:1–5)

God saw what they had done, that they had turned away from their evil lives. He *did* change his mind about them. What he said he would do to them he didn't do. (3:10)

Jonah was furious. He lost his temper. He yelled at God, "God! I knew it—when I was back home, I knew this was going to happen! That's why I ran off to Tarshish! I knew you were sheer grace and mercy, not easily angered, rich in love, and ready at the drop of a hat to turn your plans of punishment into a program of forgiveness!

"So, GOD, if you won't kill them, kill *me*! I'm better off dead!"

GOD said, "What do you have to be angry about?"

But Jonah just left. He went out of the city to the east and sat down in a sulk. He put together a makeshift shelter of leafy branches and sat there in the shade to see what would happen to the city.

GOD arranged for a broad-leafed tree to spring up. It grew over Jonah to cool him off and get him out of his angry sulk. Jonah was pleased and enjoyed the shade. Life was looking up.

But then God sent a worm. By dawn of the next day, the worm had bored into the shade tree and it withered away. The sun came up and God sent a hot, blistering wind from the east. The sun beat down on Jonah's head and he started to faint. He prayed to die: "I'm better off dead!"

Then God said to Jonah, "What right do you have to get angry about this shade tree?"

Jonah said, "Plenty of right. It's made me angry enough to die!"

GOD said, "What's this? How is it that you can change your feelings from pleasure to anger overnight about a mere shade tree that you did nothing to get? You neither planted nor watered it. It grew up one night and died the next night. So, why can't I likewise change what I feel about Nineveh from anger to pleasure, this big city of more than 120,000 child-like people who don't yet know right from wrong, to say nothing of all the innocent animals?" (Jonah 4)

TALK ABOUT IT

- Why did Jonah get swallowed up by the giant fish?
- How do you feel when someone who has done something wrong gets caught? Why did Jonah get angry?
- How did God demonstrate his love and mercy in today's story?
- Is there anything that confuses you about this story? If so, it's okay! Do you have any questions about Jonah? It's time to ask your questions about the Bible.

CLOSING THOUGHT

Jonah is another example of people being more concerned about justice than they are about love. God sent Jonah to warn the Ninevites they were going to be in big trouble if they didn't shape up. When they took Jonah's message seriously, it made Jonah really frustrated. He didn't want God to be merciful, he wanted God to punish the Ninevites! But God gave them the chance to repent, or change, their ways.

God is a God of second, third, fourth, and fifth chances. He is patient with both Jonah and the Ninevites, willing to show them *both* the way of loving kindness and mercy. He is ready to change his mind and forgive the wrongs of anyone who has a change of heart—even the people of Nineveh, and even Jonah.

PRAYER PROMPT

Pray Psalm 138 (MSG) below, a psalm of thanksgiving for all that God has done:

> Thank you! Everything in me says "Thank you!"
>   Angels listen as I sing my thanks.
> I kneel in worship facing your holy temple
>   and say it again: "Thank you!"
> Thank you for your love,
>   thank you for your faithfulness;
> Most holy is your name,
>   most holy is your Word.
> The moment I called out, you stepped in;
>   you made my life large with strength.
>
> When they hear what you have to say, GOD,
>   all earth's kings will say "Thank you."
> They'll sing of what you've done:
>   "How great the glory of GOD!"
> And here's why: GOD, high above, sees far below;
>   no matter the distance, he knows everything about us.

When I walk into the thick of trouble,
  keep me alive in the angry turmoil.
With one hand
  strike my foes,
With your other hand
  save me.
Finish what you started in me, GOD.
  Your love is eternal—don't quit on me now.

ACTIVITY #1: THE BIG FISH!

Create a "big fish" in your living room. Couch cushions, some blankets hung over chairs, and maybe cardboard will be needed. Get creative! In today's story Jonah spent three days in the belly of the fish praying. Crawl inside your fish. What will you pray for?

ACTIVITY #2: LOVE FOR NINEVEH

Show God's love to those who are on the outskirts of society. What ministries does your church support to reach the hungry, the poor, the homeless, the imprisoned, and the shut-ins (a shut-in is someone who is homebound and can't leave because they are too ill)? Do something to show God's love to them this week.

Nineveh and the Queen of Sheba

In Matthew 12:38–45, Jesus points to the people of Nineveh and the Queen of Sheba as the people who will speak up at the end of days about God. Nineveh was an ancient city situated in modern-day Iraq, and Sheba was an ancient kingdom in the Middle East near Africa (probably in the country of Yemen today). Neither the people of Nineveh nor the Queen of Sheba were Jewish. They didn't come by their faith because of their skin tone or their ancestry. They came to faith by pursuing God with a humble heart and a spirit ready to receive God's mercy and correction.

Jesus and Nicodemus

SETTING UP THE STORY

We've been reading about people who are more interested in God's judgment than God's mercy. Jesus has some strong words for them. But the people who struggle to see God's grace aren't doomed to be separate from that love. Even the religious leaders (and those like Jonah) who might be missing the point of Jesus's message can receive God's love. In today's story, Jesus meets with one such man.

READ: JOHN 3:1–21 (MSG)

There was a man of the Pharisee sect, Nicodemus, a prominent leader among the Jews. Late one night he visited Jesus and said, "Rabbi, we all know you're a teacher straight from God. No one could do all the God-pointing, God-revealing acts you do if God weren't in on it."

Jesus said, "You're absolutely right. Take it from me: Unless a person is born from above, it's not possible to see what I'm pointing to—to God's kingdom."

"How can anyone," said Nicodemus, "be born who has already been born and grown up? You can't re-enter your mother's womb and be born again. What are you saying with this 'born-from-above' talk?"

Jesus said, "You're not listening. Let me say it again. Unless a person submits to this original creation—the 'wind-hovering-over-the-water' creation, the invisible moving the visible, a baptism into a new life—it's not possible to enter God's kingdom. When you look at a baby, it's just that: a body you can look at and touch. But the person who takes shape within is formed by something you can't see and touch—the Spirit—and becomes a living spirit.

"So don't be so surprised when I tell you that you have to be 'born from above'—out of this world, so to speak. You know well enough how the wind blows this way and that. You hear it rustling through the trees, but you have no idea where it comes from or where it's headed next. That's the way it is with everyone 'born from above' by the wind of God, the Spirit of God."

Nicodemus asked, "What do you mean by this? How does this happen?"

Jesus said, "You're a respected teacher of Israel and you don't know these basics? Listen carefully. I'm speaking sober truth to you. I speak only of what I know by experience; I give witness only to what I have seen with my own eyes. There is nothing secondhand here, no hearsay. Yet instead of facing the evidence and accepting it, you procrastinate with questions. If I tell you things that are plain as the hand before your face and you don't believe me, what use is there in telling you of things you can't see, the things of God?

"No one has ever gone up into the presence of God except the One who came down from that Presence, the Son of Man. In the same way that Moses lifted the serpent in the desert so people could have something to see and then believe, it is necessary for the Son of Man to be lifted up—and everyone who looks up to him, trusting and expectant, will gain a real life, eternal life.

"This is how much God loved the world: He gave his Son, his one and only Son. And this is why: so that no one need be destroyed; by believing in him, anyone can have a whole and lasting life. God didn't go to all the trouble of sending his Son merely to point an accusing finger, telling the world how bad it was. He came to help, to put the world right again. Anyone who trusts in him is acquitted; anyone who refuses to trust him has long since been under the death sentence without knowing it. And why? Because of that person's failure to believe in the one-of-a-kind Son of God when introduced to him.

"This is the crisis we're in: God-light streamed into the world, but men and women everywhere ran for the darkness. They went for the darkness because they were not really interested in pleasing God. Everyone who makes a practice of doing evil, addicted to denial and illusion, hates God-light and won't come near it, fearing a painful exposure. But anyone working and living in truth and reality welcomes God-light so the work can be seen for the God-work it is."

TALK ABOUT IT

- Why do you think Nicodemus came to Jesus at night?
- What do you think Jesus meant by needing to be "born from above"?
- What does it mean to you to know that Jesus came to give a whole and lasting life?
- This passage says that God "came to help, to put the world right again." What does this tell you about God?
- Is there anything about Jesus that confuses you? Is there anything that is hard to believe? Don't be afraid to share. Do you have any questions about John 3:1–21? It's time to ask your questions about the Bible.

CLOSING THOUGHT

Anyone who has doubts about God, or questions about being a Christian that are hard to answer, can take comfort in Nicodemus's story. Nicodemus had been taught a specific way of understanding God and didn't understand Jesus's message. But there was something about Jesus that just wouldn't let him go.

After Jesus died, Nicodemus joined Joseph of Arimathea (a secret follower of Jesus) when it was time to bury Jesus (John 19:38–42). The two men brought about seventy-five pounds' worth of spices for his burial—a common method of honoring and respecting the person who died (see John 19:39)—and buried Jesus in Joseph's tomb. All throughout Jesus's ministry, the truth of Jesus's words must have stuck with Nicodemus.

Jesus welcomes all who seek after him, even those who struggle with faith. God's light shines even through our doubt; all we have to do is walk into it.

PRAYER PROMPT

Thank God for waiting patiently with us, no matter what questions we have. Thank God for the ways he blesses people. What ways has God blessed your life? Thank God for that today.

ACTIVITY: BLESS THE TEACHERS

Nicodemus was one of the religious leaders during the time of Jesus, and even he struggled in his faith. The priests, pastors, and teachers that we look up to in our churches might sometimes feel like Nicodemus too, quietly questioning their Savior. Do something to encourage your pastor, priest, or Sunday school teacher this week.

Moses and the Serpent in the Desert

Jesus referenced a strange passage of Scripture about Moses when talking with Nicodemus, a passage from Numbers 21:4–9 (MSG):

> They set out from Mount Hor along the Red Sea Road, a detour around the land of Edom. The people became irritable and cross as they traveled. They spoke out against God and Moses: "Why did you drag us out of Egypt to die in this godforsaken country? No decent food; no water—we can't stomach this stuff any longer."
>
> So GOD sent poisonous snakes among the people; they bit them and many in Israel died. The people came to Moses and said, "We sinned when we spoke out against GOD and you. Pray to GOD; ask him to take these snakes from us."
>
> Moses prayed for the people.
>
> GOD said to Moses, "Make a snake and put it on a flagpole: Whoever is bitten and looks at it will live."
>
> So Moses made a snake of fiery copper and put it on top of a flagpole. Anyone bitten by a snake who then looked at the copper snake lived.

Jesus said that, just like this story, the Son of Man would be lifted up, and all who look upon him, "trusting and expectant, will gain a real life, eternal life." Jesus's sacrifice on the cross removes the poison of sin from our hearts and gives us new life.

Shadrach, Meshach, and Abednego: No Other God Can Save This Way!

SETTING UP THE STORY

Today's story takes place about two hundred and fifty years *after* Elijah confronted King Ahab, and hundreds of years *before* Jesus appeared. It's the lowest point of Israel's history in the Old Testament. The Israelites had been defeated by other nations, the temple Solomon built was destroyed, and they were kicked out of the Promised Land. Many were captured and taken to Babylon by King Nebuchadnezzar. None of the people around the Israelites followed God. They also didn't like that the Israelites followed a god other than theirs. In today's story, God shows his power over the foreign gods in miraculous ways.

READ: DANIEL 3 (NIV)

King Nebuchadnezzar made an image of gold, sixty cubits high and six cubits wide, and set it up on the plain of Dura in the province of Babylon. He then summoned the satraps, prefects, governors, advisers, treasurers, judges, magistrates and all the other provincial officials to come to the dedication of the image he had set up. So the satraps, prefects, governors, advisers, treasurers, judges, magistrates and all the other provincial officials assembled for the dedication of the image that King Nebuchadnezzar had set up, and they stood before it.

Then the herald loudly proclaimed, "Nations and peoples of every language, this is what you are commanded to do: As soon as you hear the sound of the horn, flute, zither, lyre, harp, pipe and all kinds of music, you must fall down and worship the image of gold that King Nebuchadnezzar has set up. Whoever does not fall down and worship will immediately be thrown into a blazing furnace."

Therefore, as soon as they heard the sound of the horn, flute, zither, lyre, harp and all kinds of music, all the nations and peoples of every language fell down and worshiped the image of gold that King Nebuchadnezzar had set up.

At this time some astrologers came forward and denounced the Jews. They said to King Nebuchadnezzar, "May the king live forever! Your Majesty has issued a decree that everyone who hears the sound of the horn, flute, zither, lyre, harp, pipe and all kinds of music must fall down and worship the image of gold, and that whoever does not fall down and worship will be thrown into a blazing furnace. But there are some Jews whom you have set over the affairs of the province of Babylon—Shadrach, Meshach and Abednego—who pay no attention to you, Your Majesty. They neither serve your gods nor worship the image of gold you have set up."

Furious with rage, Nebuchadnezzar summoned Shadrach, Meshach and Abednego. So these men were brought before the king, and Nebuchadnezzar said to them, "Is it true, Shadrach, Meshach and Abednego, that you do not serve my gods or worship the image of gold I have set up? Now when you hear the sound of the horn, flute, zither, lyre, harp, pipe and all kinds of music, if you are ready to fall down and worship the image I made, very good. But if you do not worship it, you will be thrown immediately into a blazing furnace. Then what god will be able to rescue you from my hand?"

Shadrach, Meshach and Abednego replied to him, "King Nebuchadnezzar, we do not need to defend ourselves before you in this matter. If we are thrown into the blazing furnace, the God we serve is able to deliver us from it, and he will deliver us from Your Majesty's hand. But even if he does not, we want you to know, Your Majesty, that we will not serve your gods or worship the image of gold you have set up."

Then Nebuchadnezzar was furious with Shadrach, Meshach and Abednego, and his attitude toward them changed. He ordered the furnace heated seven times hotter than usual and commanded some of the strongest soldiers in his army to tie up Shadrach, Meshach and Abednego and throw them into the blazing furnace. So these men, wearing their robes, trousers, turbans and other clothes, were bound and thrown into the blazing furnace. The king's command was so urgent and the furnace so hot that the flames of the fire killed the soldiers who took up Shadrach, Meshach and Abednego, and these three men, firmly tied, fell into the blazing furnace.

Then King Nebuchadnezzar leaped to his feet in amazement and asked his advisers, "Weren't there three men that we tied up and threw into the fire?"

They replied, "Certainly, Your Majesty."

He said, "Look! I see four men walking around in the fire, unbound and unharmed, and the fourth looks like a son of the gods."

Nebuchadnezzar then approached the opening of the blazing furnace and shouted, "Shadrach, Meshach and Abednego, servants of the Most High God, come out! Come here!"

So Shadrach, Meshach and Abednego came out of the fire, and the satraps, prefects, governors and royal advisers crowded around them. They saw that the fire had not harmed their bodies, nor was a hair of their heads singed; their robes were not scorched, and there was no smell of fire on them.

Then Nebuchadnezzar said, "Praise be to the God of Shadrach, Meshach and Abednego, who has sent his angel and rescued his servants! They trusted in him and defied the king's command and were willing to give up their lives rather than serve or worship any god except their own God. Therefore I decree that the people of any nation or language who say anything against the God of Shadrach, Meshach and Abednego be cut into pieces and their houses be turned into piles of rubble, for no other god can save in this way."

Then the king promoted Shadrach, Meshach and Abednego in the province of Babylon.

TALK ABOUT IT

- What was it King Nebuchadnezzar demanded of all of the people?
- Why didn't the Israelites do it?

- How does God rescue Shadrach, Meshach, and Abednego?
- Who do you think was in the fire with them?
- How do you think the three men in today's story felt?
- Is there anything that confuses you about this story? If so, it's okay! Do you have any questions about Daniel 3? It's time to ask your questions about the Bible.

CLOSING THOUGHT

People around the world face the very real fear of punishment or death for following Jesus. Even if you aren't in a place that threatens your physical well-being for believing and worshipping Jesus, there are still many times every day when we have to make a decision—whether to go along with what's popular or whether to stand up for what's right. God gives us his Holy Spirit to help us figure out what is good, and he's given us his Word to guide us toward what's right. He showed us through Jesus what it looks like to be holy, and holiness looks like peace, kindness, mercy, patience, and love.

PRAYER PROMPT

Pray for the courage to stand up for what is right. Thank God that no matter what you encounter every day, he is with you and loves you deeply. Take turns offering up your prayer to God today.

ACTIVITY: IMMIGRANTS AND REFUGEES

The Israelites lived in a foreign land, among people with a different way of life. When people have to leave their home countries today, they face all kinds of challenges. For example, sometimes the new country where they settle doesn't speak the same language. The foods they were accustomed to at home aren't always readily available at the local grocery store. If they left their countries because of war or oppression, they might not have been able to bring much with them. Are there refugees and immigrants living near you? If so, find out what their needs are and put together a basket of resources to show you care. There are often organizations in communities to help immigrants and refugees find work, resources, homes, and more to help them get to know the local area.

King Nebuchadnezzar and Babylon

The book of Daniel was written about four hundred years after the time that King Nebuchadnezzar ruled in Babylon, during a time when the Israelites were under oppression by another foreign government. Nebuchadnezzar ruled over Babylon for over forty years, conquering surrounding kingdoms, including Jerusalem, and building up his empire. The kingdom of Babylon must have been very large and ornate. Its ruins are spread out over two thousand acres, making it the largest archaeological site in the Middle East.

Lazarus, Come Out!

SETTING UP THE STORY

SETTING UP THE STORY

Last time we read about how God saved Shadrach, Meshach, and Abednego from the fiery furnace. Today, we'll learn about another time when God saved and see how Jesus responded to the death of one of his closest friends.

READ: JOHN 11:1–44 (NLT)

A man named Lazarus was sick. He lived in Bethany with his sisters, Mary and Martha. This is the Mary who later poured the expensive perfume on the Lord's feet and wiped them with her hair. Her brother, Lazarus, was sick. So the two sisters sent a message to Jesus telling him, "Lord, your dear friend is very sick."

But when Jesus heard about it he said, "Lazarus's sickness will not end in death. No, it happened for the glory of God so that the Son of God will receive glory from this." So although Jesus loved Martha, Mary, and Lazarus, he stayed where he was for the next two days. Finally, he said to his disciples, "Let's go back to Judea."

But his disciples objected. "Rabbi," they said, "only a few days ago the people in Judea were trying to stone you. Are you going there again?"

Jesus replied, "There are twelve hours of daylight every day. During the day people can walk safely. They can see because they have the light of this world. But at night there is danger of stumbling because they have no light." Then he said, "Our friend Lazarus has fallen asleep, but now I will go and wake him up."

The disciples said, "Lord, if he is sleeping, he will soon get better!" They thought Jesus meant Lazarus was simply sleeping, but Jesus meant Lazarus had died.

So he told them plainly, "Lazarus is dead. And for your sakes, I'm glad I wasn't there, for now you will really believe. Come, let's go see him."

Thomas, nicknamed the Twin, said to his fellow disciples, "Let's go, too—and die with Jesus."

When Jesus arrived at Bethany, he was told that Lazarus had already been in his grave for four days. Bethany was only a few miles down the road from Jerusalem, and many of the people had come to console Martha and Mary in their loss. When Martha got word that Jesus was coming, she went to meet him. But Mary stayed in the house. Martha said to Jesus, "Lord, if only you had been here, my brother would not have died. But even now I know that God will give you whatever you ask."

Jesus told her, "Your brother will rise again."

"Yes," Martha said, "he will rise when everyone else rises, at the last day."

Jesus told her, "I am the resurrection and the life. Anyone who believes in me will live, even after dying. Everyone who lives in me and believes in me will never ever die. Do you believe this, Martha?"

"Yes, Lord," she told him. "I have always believed you are the Messiah, the Son of God, the one who has come into the world from God." Then she returned to Mary. She called Mary aside from the mourners and told her, "The Teacher is here and wants to see you." So Mary immediately went to him.

Jesus had stayed outside the village, at the place where Martha met him. When the people who were at the house consoling Mary saw her leave so hastily, they assumed she was going to Lazarus's grave to weep. So they followed her there. When Mary arrived and saw Jesus, she fell at his feet and said, "Lord, if only you had been here, my brother would not have died."

When Jesus saw her weeping and saw the other people wailing with her, a deep anger welled up within him, and he was deeply troubled. "Where have you put him?" he asked them.

They told him, "Lord, come and see." Then Jesus wept. The people who were standing nearby said, "See how much he loved him!" But some said, "This man healed a blind man. Couldn't he have kept Lazarus from dying?"

Jesus was still angry as he arrived at the tomb, a cave with a stone rolled across its entrance. "Roll the stone aside," Jesus told them.

But Martha, the dead man's sister, protested, "Lord, he has been dead for four days. The smell will be terrible."

Jesus responded, "Didn't I tell you that you would see God's glory if you believe?" So they rolled the stone aside. Then Jesus looked up to heaven and said, "Father, thank you for hearing me. You always hear me, but I said it out loud for the sake of all these people standing here, so that they will believe you sent me." Then Jesus shouted, "Lazarus, come out!" And the dead man came out, his hands and feet bound in graveclothes, his face wrapped in a headcloth. Jesus told them, "Unwrap him and let him go!"

TALK ABOUT IT

- Why do you think Jesus didn't go to see Lazarus right before he died?
- What did Jesus's disciples think about this plan to go back to Judea and see Lazarus?
- How do you think Mary and Martha felt about Jesus during this story?
- Why do you think Jesus got angry and troubled when he saw all of the people mourning Lazarus?
- If you had watched a dead person come alive again, how do you think you'd react?
- Is there anything that confuses you about this story? If so, it's okay! Do you have any questions about John 11:1–44? It's time to ask your questions about the Bible.

CLOSING THOUGHT

Immediately after Jesus raised Lazarus from the dead, the Pharisees heard about it. They talked among themselves about what might happen soon if Jesus wasn't stopped: "This man certainly performs many miraculous signs. If we allow him to go on like this, soon everyone will believe in him. Then the Roman army will come and destroy both our Temple and our nation"

(John 11:47–48 NLT). Instead of seeing what Jesus was doing and believing that he was the Son of God, the Pharisees plotted to kill him.

Some people heard the news of Jesus and read the stories of how he healed people but they still turned away. The Pharisees were afraid of how the Romans would respond, but what happened when Shadrach, Meshach, and Abednego wouldn't worship the god of King Nebuchadnezzar? God protected them. God's love is bigger than anything frightening, scary, or mean. God's grace extends even beyond the grave!

PRAYER PROMPT

Pray that no matter what we encounter, we would rely on God, turning to his love and his grace to carry us through.

ACTIVITY: LAZARUS, COME OUT!

Act out the story of Lazarus! Take turns being Jesus, one of the disciples, Mary/Martha, and Lazarus (if you don't have enough family members for all of the roles, act out the story in parts beginning with Jesus and the disciples, then Mary/Martha and Jesus, then Jesus and Lazarus). Have fun with Lazarus and his grave clothes.

Mary and the Perfume

At the beginning of today's story, John explains that the Mary we're reading about today is the same one who put perfume on Jesus's feet. What is that all about? Shortly after Jesus raised Lazarus from the dead, "Mary took a twelve-ounce jar of expensive perfume made from essence of nard, and she anointed Jesus's feet with it, wiping his feet with her hair. The house was filled with the fragrance" (John 12:3 NLT). Judas, the disciple who betrayed Jesus later, complained that the perfume could have been sold and the money donated to the poor. But Jesus told Judas that Mary did this in preparation for his own burial. It was a generous gift that Jesus received with love. You can read the whole story in John 12:1–8.

For Such a Time as This:
Esther and Xerxes

SETTING UP THE STORY

After the Israelites were exiled in Babylon, another nation became powerful—the Persian empire. Again, the Israelites had to wrestle with how to be a people of God among people who were not Jewish and did not follow God. Today, we'll meet Esther, a Jewish orphan in exile who became queen of Persia by marrying King Xerxes. Esther's cousin, Mordecai, was both her adoptive father and a member of Xerxes's leadership (as chief minister). When Xerxes chose Esther as his queen, he didn't know she was Jewish. Haman, another person in Xerxes's court, wanted to destroy the Jewish people because Mordecai wouldn't bow down and honor him. Let's find out what happened.

READ: EXCERPTS FROM THE BOOK OF ESTHER (MSG)

Haman then spoke with King Xerxes: "There is an odd set of people scattered through the provinces of your kingdom who don't fit in. Their customs and ways are different from those of everybody else. Worse, they disregard the king's laws. They're an affront; the king shouldn't put up with them. If it please the king, let orders be given that they be destroyed. I'll pay for it myself. I'll deposit 375 tons of silver in the royal bank to finance the operation."

The king slipped his signet ring from his hand and gave it to Haman son of Hammedatha the Agagite, archenemy of the Jews.

"Go ahead," the king said to Haman. "It's your money—do whatever you want with those people." (Esther 3:8–11)

When Mordecai learned what had been done, he ripped his clothes to shreds and put on sackcloth and ashes. Then he went out in the streets of the city crying out in loud and bitter cries. He came only as far as the King's Gate, for no one dressed in sackcloth was allowed to enter the King's Gate. As the king's order was posted in every province, there was loud lament among the Jews—fasting, weeping, wailing. And most of them stretched out on sackcloth and ashes.

Esther's maids and eunuchs came and told her. The queen was stunned. She sent fresh clothes to Mordecai so he could take off his sackcloth but he wouldn't accept them. Esther called for Hathach, one of the royal eunuchs whom the king had assigned to wait on her, and told him to go to Mordecai and get the full story of what was happening. So Hathach went to Mordecai in the town square in front of the King's Gate. Mordecai told him everything that had happened to him. He also told him the exact amount of money that Haman had promised to deposit in the royal bank to finance the massacre of the Jews. Mordecai also gave him a copy of the bulletin that had been posted in Susa ordering the massacre so he could show it to Esther when he reported back with instructions to go to the king and intercede and plead with him for her people.

Hathach came back and told Esther everything Mordecai had said. Esther talked it over with Hathach and then sent him back to Mordecai with this message: "Everyone who works for the king here, and even the people out in the provinces, knows that there is a single fate for every man or woman who approaches the king without being invited: death. The one exception is if the king extends his gold scepter; then he or she may live. And it's been thirty days now since I've been invited to come to the king."

When Hathach told Mordecai what Esther had said, Mordecai sent her this message: "Don't think that just because you live in the king's house you're the one Jew who will get out of this alive. If you persist in staying silent at a time like this, help and deliverance will arrive for the Jews from someplace else; but you and your family will be wiped out. Who knows? Maybe you were made queen for just such a time as this."

Esther sent back her answer to Mordecai: "Go and get all the Jews living in Susa together. Fast for me. Don't eat or drink for three days, either day or night. I and my maids will fast with you. If you will do this, I'll go to the king, even though it's forbidden. If I die, I die."

Mordecai left and carried out Esther's instructions. (Esther 4)

So the king and Haman went to dinner with Queen Esther. At this second dinner, while they were drinking wine the king again asked, "Queen Esther, what would you like? Half of my kingdom! Just ask and it's yours."

Queen Esther answered, "If I have found favor in your eyes, O King, and if it please the king, give me my life, and give my people their lives.

"We've been sold, I and my people, to be destroyed—sold to be massacred, eliminated. If we had just been sold off into slavery, I wouldn't even have brought it up; our troubles wouldn't have been worth bothering the king over."

King Xerxes exploded, "Who? Where is he? This is monstrous!"

"An enemy. An adversary. This evil Haman," said Esther.

Haman was terror-stricken before the king and queen. (Esther 7:1–6)

That same day King Xerxes gave Queen Esther the estate of Haman, archenemy of the Jews. And Mordecai came before the king because Esther had explained their relationship. The king took off his signet ring, which he had taken back from Haman, and gave it to Mordecai. Esther appointed Mordecai over Haman's estate.

Then Esther again spoke to the king, falling at his feet, begging with tears to counter the evil of Haman the Agagite and revoke the plan that he had plotted against the Jews. The king extended his gold scepter to Esther. She got to her feet and stood before the king. She said, "If it please the king and he regards me with favor and thinks this is right, and if he has any affection for me at all, let an order be written that cancels the bulletins authorizing the plan of Haman son of Hammedatha the Agagite to annihilate the Jews in all the king's provinces. How can I stand to see this catastrophe wipe out my people? How can I bear to stand by and watch the massacre of my own relatives?"

King Xerxes said to Queen Esther and Mordecai the Jew: "I've given Haman's estate to Esther and he's been hanged on the gallows because he attacked the Jews. So go ahead now and write whatever you decide on behalf of the Jews; then seal it with the signet ring." (An order written in the king's name and sealed with his signet ring is irrevocable.) (Esther 8:1–8)

TALK ABOUT IT

- What did Xerxes plan to allow to happen to the Jews?
- How did Esther react to Haman's plans?
- How do you think Esther felt confronting the king, knowing that she could be killed for doing so?
- Did Esther *have* to go to Xerxes? What other options did Esther have?
- Is there anything that confuses you about this story? If so, it's okay! Do you have any questions about Esther? It's time to ask your questions about the Bible.

CLOSING THOUGHT

God isn't mentioned once in today's story. He isn't talked about or brought up at all in the entire book of Esther. It is one of only two books in the whole Bible that doesn't mention God by name (the other is the Song of Songs, or the Song of Solomon). But that doesn't mean God isn't present in today's story.

Esther shows us what it's like to make good, hard decisions because of faith in God, in a place that doesn't value that faith. Mordecai told Esther that maybe she was queen for "such a time as this" (Esther 4:14). Mordecai encouraged her to put her life at risk for innocent people. Now *that's* faith.

Esther had a choice: she could risk her life and use her relationship with the king to save the Jewish people, or she could ignore Mordecai and live happily in the king's palace. She chose to speak with Xerxes. She didn't know if God would protect her from death or not, but she trusted God *to be with her* no matter what.

PRAYER PROMPT

There are people all over the world who find themselves under governments that do not allow them to talk about their faith in God. Pray for their courage and strength to walk with God even under threat. Pray for God to give you the same courage and strength to live out your trust in God where you live.

ACTIVITY: BE AN ADVOCATE

Esther went to the powers that be to stand up for her people, even though it meant potentially suffering severe consequences. She had a voice and spoke the power of God's love to leadership. Write a letter to your leaders (school leaders, work leaders, church leaders, or government leaders) to tell them God loves them.

What Is a Signet Ring?

Xerxes gave Haman and then Mordecai his signet ring as a commitment to doing as he said. The signet ring is like a signature today—it is a sign of a promise made. In ancient times, people of authority would give their signet ring to a messenger to prove that the message they were sending was true and real. They would also use it to seal messages by pressing the ring into melted wax. God calls the Jewish people (particularly David's descendants) his signet ring through the prophet Haggai (see Haggai 2:23). It's through the Jewish people that God would send *his* messenger to prove that *his* message was true and real—and that messenger was Jesus!

One Bright Morning: Mary Magdalene and Jesus at the Tomb

SETTING UP THE STORY

Our last few stories have focused on God as Deliverer. *Deliverer* means savior, rescuer, someone who saves you from harm or danger. We saw God deliver Shadrach, Meshach, and Abednego from the fire. We saw God deliver the Jews from Xerxes through Esther. And we saw God deliver Lazarus, Martha, and Mary from death and grief. Each of these stories could have ended in despair, but God delivered hope instead. Today, we'll read about the ultimate sign of the hope that we have in Jesus.

READ: JOHN 20:1–18 (NIV)

Early on the first day of the week, while it was still dark, Mary Magdalene went to the tomb and saw that the stone had been removed from the entrance. So she came running to Simon Peter and the other disciple, the one Jesus loved, and said, "They have taken the Lord out of the tomb, and we don't know where they have put him!"

So Peter and the other disciple started for the tomb. Both were running, but the other disciple outran Peter and reached the tomb first. He bent over and looked in at the strips of linen lying there but did not go in. Then Simon Peter came along behind him and went straight into the tomb. He saw the strips of linen lying there, as well as the cloth that had been wrapped around Jesus' head. The cloth was still lying in its place, separate from the linen. Finally the other disciple, who had reached the tomb first, also went inside. He saw and believed. (They still did not understand from Scripture that Jesus had to rise from the dead.) Then the disciples went back to where they were staying.

Now Mary stood outside the tomb crying. As she wept, she bent over to look into the tomb and saw two angels in white, seated where Jesus' body had been, one at the head and the other at the foot.

They asked her, "Woman, why are you crying?"

"They have taken my Lord away," she said, "and I don't know where they have put him." At this, she turned around and saw Jesus standing there, but she did not realize that it was Jesus.

He asked her, "Woman, why are you crying? Who is it you are looking for?"

Thinking he was the gardener, she said, "Sir, if you have carried him away, tell me where you have put him, and I will get him."

Jesus said to her, "Mary."

She turned toward him and cried out in Aramaic, "Rabboni!" (which means "Teacher").

Jesus said, "Do not hold on to me, for I have not yet ascended to the Father. Go instead to my brothers and tell them, 'I am ascending to my Father and your Father, to my God and your God.'"

Mary Magdalene went to the disciples with the news: "I have seen the Lord!" And she told them that he had said these things to her.

TALK ABOUT IT

- Before his death, did Jesus tell the disciples what was going to happen to him?
- If you had been "the one Jesus loved" at the tomb, how would you have felt?
- Why do you think Mary didn't recognize Jesus?
- Earlier in the Gospel stories, Jesus cast out seven demons from Mary Magdalene. Why do you think Jesus chose to reveal himself to her instead of Peter, John, or one of the other apostles?
- Is there anything that confuses you about this story? If so, it's okay! Do you have any questions about John 20:1–18? It's time to ask your questions about the Bible.

CLOSING THOUGHT

Mary Magdalene had experienced a grace that the other disciples hadn't felt yet. When Jesus cast out seven demons from her, she was delivered, saved, and rescued from darkness (Luke 8:2). Jesus was her Savior even before he died and rose again. His death would have shattered Mary because the man who had saved her was gone.

When Jesus appeared to Mary he restored her hope. First Jesus delivered her from demons, then he delivered Lazarus from the grave, and now Jesus conquered death itself! Jesus's resurrection is the signet ring, or stamp of authority, that all Jesus said and did on earth was truly God's Word, that God's relationship with us is not one of condemnation but of unconditional love.

PRAYER PROMPT

Let's pray that God's hope would be ever-present for us today. Pray for healing for those who grieve. And pray that the hope of eternal life would bring comfort to all.

ACTIVITY: TOMB THEATER

Act out today's story with your family, taking turns being the different characters. What emotions would each of the characters have felt? How would they have interacted? How would their expressions have changed when Jesus showed up?

Mary Magdalene

Mary Magdalene was a Jewish woman who had seven demons cast out of her by Jesus and became one of his closest followers. She is named throughout the four Gospels at least twelve times, more than most of the apostles. She was a witness to Jesus's crucifixion and was the first to see Jesus after his resurrection.

Tongues of Fire, Changed Lives

SETTING UP THE STORY

The apostles who followed Jesus for three years before he died were constantly bewildered by Jesus. What Jesus said and did was so different than what they had heard for years from their religious leaders. When Jesus was in his moment of greatest need, they all fled. But after Jesus was resurrected, a new courage came upon the apostles. Imagine what it must have been like to see Jesus, risen from the grave! Let's find out what happened on the day of Pentecost.

READ: ACTS 2 (NLT)

On the day of Pentecost all the believers were meeting together in one place. Suddenly, there was a sound from heaven like the roaring of a mighty windstorm, and it filled the house where they were sitting. Then, what looked like flames or tongues of fire appeared and settled on each of them. And everyone present was filled with the Holy Spirit and began speaking in other languages, as the Holy Spirit gave them this ability.

At that time there were devout Jews from every nation living in Jerusalem. When they heard the loud noise, everyone came running, and they were bewildered to hear their own languages being spoken by the believers.

They were completely amazed. "How can this be?" they exclaimed. "These people are all from Galilee, and yet we hear them speaking in our own native languages! Here we are—Parthians, Medes, Elamites, people from Mesopotamia, Judea, Cappadocia, Pontus, the province of Asia, Phrygia, Pamphylia, Egypt, and the areas of Libya around Cyrene, visitors from Rome (both Jews and converts to Judaism), Cretans, and Arabs. And we all hear these people speaking in our own languages about the wonderful things God has done!" They stood there amazed and perplexed. "What can this mean?" they asked each other.

But others in the crowd ridiculed them, saying, "They're just drunk, that's all!"

Then Peter stepped forward with the eleven other apostles and shouted to the crowd, "Listen carefully, all of you, fellow Jews and residents of Jerusalem! Make no mistake about this. These people are not drunk, as some of you are assuming. Nine o'clock in the morning is much too early for that. No, what you see was predicted long ago by the prophet Joel:

'In the last days,' God says,

'I will pour out my Spirit upon all people.
Your sons and daughters will prophesy.
   Your young men will see visions,
   and your old men will dream dreams.
In those days I will pour out my Spirit
   even on my servants—men and women alike—
   and they will prophesy.
And I will cause wonders in the heavens above
   and signs on the earth below—
   blood and fire and clouds of smoke.
The sun will become dark,
   and the moon will turn blood red
   before that great and glorious day of the LORD arrives.
But everyone who calls on the name of the LORD
   will be saved.'

"People of Israel, listen! God publicly endorsed Jesus the Nazarene by doing powerful miracles, wonders, and signs through him, as you well know. But God knew what would happen, and his prearranged plan was carried out when Jesus was betrayed. With the help of lawless Gentiles, you nailed him to a cross and killed him. But God released him from the horrors of death and raised him back to life, for death could not keep him in its grip. King David said this about him:

'I see that the LORD is always with me.

I will not be shaken, for he is right beside me.

No wonder my heart is glad,

and my tongue shouts his praises!

My body rests in hope.

For you will not leave my soul among the dead

or allow your Holy One to rot in the grave.

You have shown me the way of life,

and you will fill me with the joy of your presence.'

"Dear brothers, think about this! You can be sure that the patriarch David wasn't referring to himself, for he died and was buried, and his tomb is still here among us. But he was a prophet, and he knew God had promised with an oath that one of David's own descendants would sit on his throne. David was looking into the future and speaking of the Messiah's resurrection. He was saying that God would not leave him among the dead or allow his body to rot in the grave.

"God raised Jesus from the dead, and we are all witnesses of this. Now he is exalted to the place of highest honor in heaven, at God's right hand. And the Father, as he had promised, gave him the Holy Spirit to pour out upon us, just as you see and hear today. For David himself never ascended into heaven, yet he said,

'The LORD said to my Lord,

"Sit in the place of honor at my right hand

until I humble your enemies,

making them a footstool under your feet."'

"So let everyone in Israel know for certain that God has made this Jesus, whom you crucified, to be both Lord and Messiah!"

Peter's words pierced their hearts, and they said to him and to the other apostles, "Brothers, what should we do?"

Peter replied, "Each of you must repent of your sins and turn to God, and be baptized in the name of Jesus Christ for the forgiveness of your sins. Then you will receive the gift of the Holy Spirit. This promise is to you, to your children, and to those far away—all who have been called by the Lord our God." Then Peter continued preaching for a long time, strongly urging all his listeners, "Save yourselves from this crooked generation!"

Those who believed what Peter said were baptized and added to the church that day—about 3,000 in all.

All the believers devoted themselves to the apostles' teaching, and to fellowship, and to sharing in meals (including the Lord's Supper), and to prayer.

A deep sense of awe came over them all, and the apostles performed many miraculous signs and wonders. And all the believers met together in one place and shared everything they had. They sold their property and possessions and shared the money with those in need. They worshiped together at the Temple each day, met in homes for the Lord's Supper, and shared their meals with great joy and generosity—all the while praising God and enjoying the goodwill of all the people. And each day the Lord added to their fellowship those who were being saved.

TALK ABOUT IT

- What do you think a "tongue of fire" looks like? Can you picture it?
- What convinced the people around the apostles that Jesus was Lord?
- What do you think it means that "Peter's words pierced their hearts"?
- What did the people do to show that they believed?
- Talk about the community of believers described at the end of today's story. Are you in a community of believers that looks like the early church?
- If you could experience any part of that community, what would you like most?
- Is there anything that confuses you about this story? If so, it's okay! Do you have any questions about Acts 2? It's time to ask your questions about the Bible.

CLOSING THOUGHT

The Holy Spirit's arrival had been promised by Jesus before his death: "And I will ask the Father, and he will give you another Advocate, who will never leave you. He is the Holy Spirit, who leads into all truth. The world cannot receive him, because it isn't looking for him and doesn't recognize him. But you know him, because he lives with you now and later will be in you." (John 14:16–17 NLT).

How do we know what the Spirit of God looks like among us today? By knowing who Jesus is, reading what he is like, and looking for his presence in the world. Wherever there is love, there you will find the Holy Spirit. In a dark world, love is a flaming tongue of fire, lighting the way and making the darkness flee. When we turn toward God, we naturally turn away from things that are not of God. That's where the Holy Spirit meets us, in the turning and in the constant decision to walk in his light.

PRAYER PROMPT

Praise God for his ever-present Spirit! Praise God for always being with you and for guiding you by his Spirit.

ACTIVITY #1: FEAST WITH YOUR CHRISTIAN COMMUNITY

Plan a get-together with your family and friends who are also followers of Jesus. Invite everyone to bring their favorite dish to pass (share everything in common), and as part of the get-together, ask each person there to share one thing they feel Jesus has done for them to change their lives. Celebrate the Holy Spirit's presence together and have a good time!

ACTIVITY #2: MARK THE DAY OF PENTECOST

The Day of Pentecost is observed each year by Christians around the world, yet many people are not aware of it, or don't observe it at all. With your parent's permission, find out when the next Day of Pentecost will be celebrated and mark it on a family calendar. (It's usually in the spring or early summer.) Make a note to gather as a family on this day and reread Acts 2, remembering that God sent his Spirit to guide, comfort, and empower us.

Baptism

The Jewish people had a form of baptism before Jesus's time that was a purification ritual required in order to convert to Judaism. For Christians, baptism is an important and personal moment that serves as a public symbol of our admission into God's family, adopted as his children. Different groups of Christians have different ways of performing baptisms but they all mean the same thing—we've committed to following Jesus, we've turned away from living for ourselves, we want to live out of God's love for us and for others, and we want other people to know about it.

Saul, Saul, Why Are You Out to Get Me?

SETTING UP THE STORY

Last time we read about Peter's message to the Jews at Pentecost. Peter was a major force in leading the early church after Jesus was resurrected. Today, we'll meet an unlikely leader, a guy named Saul, whose story in the Bible begins with his threatening and killing of early Christians (who called themselves "the Way"), which he thought was the right thing to do for God. Let's find out what happens to Saul and how his life is changed.

READ: ACTS 9:1–22 (MSG)

All this time Saul was breathing down the necks of the Master's disciples, out for the kill. He went to the Chief Priest and got arrest warrants to take to the meeting places in Damascus so that if he found anyone there belonging to the Way, whether men or women, he could arrest them and bring them to Jerusalem.

He set off. When he got to the outskirts of Damascus, he was suddenly dazed by a blinding flash of light. As he fell to the ground, he heard a voice: "Saul, Saul, why are you out to get me?"

He said, "Who are you, Master?"

"I am Jesus, the One you're hunting down. I want you to get up and enter the city. In the city you'll be told what to do next."

His companions stood there dumbstruck—they could hear the sound, but couldn't see anyone—while Saul, picking himself up off the ground, found himself stone-blind. They had to take him by the hand and lead him into Damascus. He continued blind for three days. He ate nothing, drank nothing.

There was a disciple in Damascus by the name of Ananias. The Master spoke to him in a vision: "Ananias."

"Yes, Master?" he answered.

"Get up and go over to Straight Avenue. Ask at the house of Judas for a man from Tarsus. His name is Saul. He's there praying. He has just had a dream in which he saw a man named Ananias enter the house and lay hands on him so he could see again."

Ananias protested, "Master, you can't be serious. Everybody's talking about this man and the terrible things he's been doing, his reign of terror against your people in Jerusalem! And now he's shown up here with papers from the Chief Priest that give him license to do the same to us."

But the Master said, "Don't argue. Go! I have picked him as my personal representative to non-Jews and kings and Jews. And now I'm about to show him what he's in for—the hard suffering that goes with this job."

So Ananias went and found the house, placed his hands on blind Saul, and said, "Brother Saul, the Master sent me, the same Jesus you saw on your way here. He sent me so you could see again and be filled with the Holy Spirit." No sooner were the words out of his mouth than something like scales fell from Saul's eyes—he could see again! He got to his feet, was baptized, and sat down with them to a hearty meal.

Saul spent a few days getting acquainted with the Damascus disciples, but then went right to work, wasting no time, preaching in the meeting places that this Jesus was the Son of God. They were caught off guard by this and, not at all sure they could trust him, they kept saying, "Isn't this the man who wreaked havoc in Jerusalem among the believers? And didn't he come here to do the same thing—arrest us and drag us off to jail in Jerusalem for sentencing by the high priests?"

But their suspicions didn't slow Saul down for even a minute. His momentum was up now and he plowed straight into the opposition, disarming the Damascus Jews and trying to show them that this Jesus was the Messiah.

TALK ABOUT IT

- What was Saul on the way to do when he met Jesus on the road to Damascus?

- How do you think Saul felt after hearing God's voice?
- Why do you think he was blind for a few days after talking with God?
- If you were Ananias, how would you have reacted to God's prompting to go talk to Saul—someone who was known for killing Jesus's followers?
- Have you ever thought what you were doing was the right thing, only to find out later what a mistake you had made? Share how that made you feel.
- Is there anything that confuses you about this story? If so, it's okay! Do you have any questions about Acts 9:1–22? It's time to ask your questions about the Bible.

CLOSING THOUGHT

The word *repent* means "to turn" or to have a dramatic change of heart. Saul sure makes a turn in today's story, from persecuting Christians to trying to show the Jews that Jesus is the Messiah!

Saul is also known as Paul. He is the writer of many of the letters to the church that are collected in the Bible. He's the kind of guy that grew up religious, knew everything there was to know about the Law, and yet like so many others throughout history, he missed God's mercy, grace, and love.

That is, until he encountered Jesus. Once he encountered Jesus, he had a dramatic change of heart. One of the things this story reveals about God is that he is capable of changing *anyone*—even violent leaders like Saul.

PRAYER PROMPT

Paul wrote in Philippians 1:9 (MSG), "So this is my prayer: that your love will flourish and that you will not only love much but well." Pray together that you will not only love much but love well.

ACTIVITY: BURNING COALS OF KINDNESS

Even knowing what Ananias knew about Saul, he still went to him in his time of need because God insisted. Later in his life Paul said this in a letter to the Romans, "Our Scriptures tell us that if you see your enemy hungry, go buy that person lunch, or if he's thirsty, get him a drink. Your generosity will surprise him with goodness. Don't let evil get the best of you; get the best of evil by doing good" (Romans 12:20–21 MSG). Is there someone who has done wrong to you? Figure out something good you can do to surprise him or her with goodness this week.

Two Names, One Man: Why Paul and Saul?

In biblical times, people were often known by different names, depending on where they were spending their time. When he was with his Hebrew friends and family, Saul would have gone by Saul, his Hebrew name. But in Greek and Roman areas, when he interacted with a lot of people who were not Jewish, Saul went by Paul, which is the name that we use most of the time when we talk about him in the Bible.[15] This happens today. People who speak other languages and come from other cultures will often take on a different name that is easier for the native speakers to understand and to say, so that their names aren't barriers to jobs or relationships.

A Different Change of Heart

SETTING UP THE STORY

Last time we saw Saul (Paul), a persecutor of the early church, experience a dramatic change of heart. Jesus's disciple, Peter, also had a big change of heart. Peter was a Jew with strong opinions about the laws of Judaism and how to follow Jesus. Sometimes he excluded people from following Jesus, or he forced them to follow Jewish rules. Let's find out what happened to Peter to cause him to change his mind about all of those rules.

READ: ACTS 10:9–43 (NIV)

About noon the following day as they were on their journey and approaching the city, Peter went up on the roof to pray. He became hungry and wanted something to eat, and while the meal was being prepared, he fell into a trance. He saw heaven opened and something like a large sheet being let down to earth by its four corners. It contained all kinds of four-footed animals, as well as reptiles and birds. Then a voice told him, "Get up, Peter. Kill and eat."

"Surely not, Lord!" Peter replied. "I have never eaten anything impure or unclean."

The voice spoke to him a second time, "Do not call anything impure that God has made clean."

This happened three times, and immediately the sheet was taken back to heaven.

While Peter was wondering about the meaning of the vision, the men sent by Cornelius found out where Simon's house was and stopped at the gate. They called out, asking if Simon who was known as Peter was staying there.

While Peter was still thinking about the vision, the Spirit said to him,

"Simon, three men are looking for you. So get up and go downstairs. Do not hesitate to go with them, for I have sent them."

Peter went down and said to the men, "I'm the one you're looking for. Why have you come?"

The men replied, "We have come from Cornelius the centurion. He is a righteous and God-fearing man, who is respected by all the Jewish people. A holy angel told him to ask you to come to his house so that he could hear what you have to say." Then Peter invited the men into the house to be his guests.

The next day Peter started out with them, and some of the believers from Joppa went along. The following day he arrived in Caesarea. Cornelius was expecting them and had called together his relatives and close friends. As Peter entered the house, Cornelius met him and fell at his feet in reverence. But Peter made him get up. "Stand up," he said, "I am only a man myself."

While talking with him, Peter went inside and found a large gathering of people. He said to them: "You are well aware that it is against our law for a Jew to associate with or visit a Gentile. But God has shown me that I should not call anyone impure or unclean. So when I was sent for, I came without raising any objection. May I ask why you sent for me?"

Cornelius answered: "Three days ago I was in my house praying at this hour, at three in the afternoon. Suddenly a man in shining clothes stood before me and said, 'Cornelius, God has heard your prayer and remembered your gifts to the poor. Send to Joppa for Simon who is called Peter. He is a guest in the home of Simon the tanner, who lives by the sea.' So I sent for you immediately, and it was good of you to come. Now we are all here in the presence of God to listen to everything the Lord has commanded you to tell us."

Then Peter began to speak: "I now realize how true it is that God does not show favoritism but accepts from every nation the one who fears him and does what is right. You know the message God sent to the people of Israel, announcing the good news of peace through Jesus Christ, who is Lord of all. You know what has happened throughout the province of Judea, beginning in Galilee after the baptism that John preached—how

God anointed Jesus of Nazareth with the Holy Spirit and power, and how he went around doing good and healing all who were under the power of the devil, because God was with him.

"We are witnesses of everything he did in the country of the Jews and in Jerusalem. They killed him by hanging him on a cross, but God raised him from the dead on the third day and caused him to be seen. He was not seen by all the people, but by witnesses whom God had already chosen—by us who ate and drank with him after he rose from the dead. He commanded us to preach to the people and to testify that he is the one whom God appointed as judge of the living and the dead. All the prophets testify about him that everyone who believes in him receives forgiveness of sins through his name."

TALK ABOUT IT

- What do you think Peter's vision of the sheet with all of the animals on it meant?
- Why was it unusual for Peter to show up at Cornelius's house?
- Is anyone prevented from receiving Jesus's forgiveness?
- Is there anything that prevents us from receiving Jesus's forgiveness?
- Is there anything that confuses you about this story? If so, it's okay! Do you have any questions about Acts 10:9–43? It's time to ask your questions about the Bible.

CLOSING THOUGHT

God is in the business of breaking down walls. All of the boundaries that men put up to keep different people apart come crashing down because of Jesus. Even though Jesus showed through his actions how God loves everyone, it still takes time and repeated messages for the idea to sink in.

For Peter, this vision and visit to Cornelius's home changed his whole world. All his life he had been told to avoid certain foods and certain people. And then he entered the home of Cornelius, a Roman soldier in charge of many other soldiers. Cornelius was a man that Peter would have *never* associated with before Jesus. He was someone to fear. Someone different. Someone *other*. But there he was, called to Cornelius's home, suddenly surrounded by all of these non-Jewish believers. And God was with them.

PRAYER PROMPT

Pray that God would open your eyes to the people you've labeled "unclean," bad, beyond saving, or just plain mean. Pray for forgiveness if you've shied away from people because they are different from you in some way. And pray for the courage and strength to love those people the way God loves you. Thank God for the grace and love that keeps pushing us forward to be more like Christ every day.

ACTIVITY: REACH OUT TO OTHERS

Go out with Jesus-colored lenses to see people through the eyes of love. Be kind, smile, and try to relate to people you otherwise might avoid just because they look, act, or speak differently than you. Talk about your experience each day together at your family's shared meals.

Unclean and Clean

The Jewish people had many rules about purity. They named certain animals as "unclean," or impure, to eat. If they ate a certain food or a certain animal, they were considered contaminated or dirty, and then they would go through a ritual to become pure again. These rules about purity extended beyond food to other areas of life. But God showed through Jesus and through the Holy Spirit that he has made all things new, all things clean.

Love Letters to the Church and Our Place in the Story

SETTING UP THE STORY

The last two lessons uncovered major changes of heart in two of the most influential leaders of the early church—Paul and Peter. Today, we'll read part of a letter from Jesus's disciple John. He wrote it to encourage the early church. Reading this letter is like opening up someone else's email from a long, long time ago. It was meant for a specific audience, but because God is bigger than us, it might just speak to you, two thousand years later.

READ: 1 JOHN 4:7–21 (NLT)

Dear friends, let us continue to love one another, for love comes from God. Anyone who loves is a child of God and knows God. But anyone who does not love does not know God, for God is love.

God showed how much he loved us by sending his one and only Son into the world so that we might have eternal life through him. This is real love—not that we loved God, but that he loved us and sent his Son as a sacrifice to take away our sins.

Dear friends, since God loved us that much, we surely ought to love each other. No one has ever seen God. But if we love each other, God lives in us, and his love is brought to full expression in us.

And God has given us his Spirit as proof that we live in him and he in us. Furthermore, we have seen with our own eyes and now testify that the Father sent his Son to be the Savior of the world. All who declare that Jesus is the Son of God have God living in them, and they live in God. We know how much God loves us, and we have put our trust in his love.

God is love, and all who live in love live in God, and God lives in them. And as we live in God, our love grows more perfect. So we will not be afraid on the day of judgment, but we can face him with confidence because we live like Jesus here in this world.

Such love has no fear, because perfect love expels all fear. If we are afraid, it is for fear of punishment, and this shows that we have not fully experienced his perfect love. We love each other because he loved us first.

If someone says, "I love God," but hates a fellow believer, that person is a liar; for if we don't love people we can see, how can we love God, whom we cannot see? And he has given us this command: Those who love God must also love their fellow believers.

TALK ABOUT IT

- According to John, how can you know if someone loves God?
- What does it mean to you to live like Jesus?
- Do you think these words from John are still true and meaningful today?
- Why do you think the people John was writing to might have needed to be reminded about what it means to love God?
- Do you feel like you need to be reminded sometimes about what it means to love God?
- Is there anything that confuses you about this story? If so, it's okay! Do you have any questions about 1 John 4:7–21? It's time to ask your questions about the Bible.

CLOSING THOUGHT

God is love. And we know God by living in love—living in love with each other, living in love with the earth, living in love with enemies, living in love with our family members, living in love with fellow believers, living every day in love. We've been reading a series of love letters. Real love isn't just rainbows and sunshine skies. Real love is sometimes difficult. Sometimes real love makes us sad or angry. Sometimes real love makes us sing and dance. Sometimes real love hurts and we suffer for it.

Real love in the Bible's story is played by Jesus, the Son of God. The words in our Bible are only ink on paper without the light and breath of love to make them come alive. And that love is carried by you. It's love that makes the Bible come alive, have meaning, and continue to speak to us. Our lives tell the story of God's love. The story doesn't end with the Bible. The story keeps being told, and will be told until God's kingdom comes. We are God's love letters.

PRAYER PROMPT

Thank God for your family members, for the loved ones who show God's love to you and to others every day. Pray for the courage and strength to live as if you are a love letter to the world.

ACTIVITY #1: WRITE A LETTER

How have you been loved? How have you loved other people? Write a letter about where you've been and what you've done. Give it to someone you love. (It would make a great gift for a grandparent.) Can you see where God is in your story? If you aren't sure, look for the places where you've felt loved, and there he'll be.

ACTIVITY #2: TELL YOUR STORY

I'm so excited that you've made it all the way to the end of this devotional! I would love to hear your story, either about this devotional, about the Bible, about church, about family life, about marriage, whatever. I believe that by telling our stories we join an ancient ritual of life-giving communion. We join together in the body of Christ to hear, to heal, to comfort, and to thrive in love, just like John encouraged the early church. Send a note to fbdstories@gmail.com sharing your story, or post to Facebook, Twitter, or Instagram and tag #FamilyBibleDevotional.

The Disciple Whom Jesus Loved

Scholars believe that John, the author of this letter, was one of the youngest apostles of Jesus. His brother, James, was also one of the apostles. The two of them were referred to by Jesus as the "Sons of Thunder" for the ways they would lose their tempers. John refers to himself as the "disciple whom Jesus loved." John is believed to be the only apostle to have died of natural causes—all of the other apostles were martyred for their faith. John is thought to be the author of the Gospel of John, the letters that use his name (1 John, 2 John, and 3 John) and the book of Revelation, which is an apocalyptic book written to encourage churches enduring intense persecution.

Notes

1. Here's a great resource for packing a care kit for the homeless: http://www.portlandrescuemission.org/get-involved/learn/pack-a-care-kit/.
2. "How Many Babies Are Born Each Day?", The World Counts, accessed February 21, 2018, http://www.theworldcounts.com/stories/How-Many-Babies-Are-Born-Each-Day.
3. Blue Letter Bible, s.v. "elohiym," accessed February 21, 2018, https://www.blueletterbible.org/lang/lexicon/lexicon.cfm?t=kjv&strongs=h430.
4. Blue Letter Bible, s. v. "Yĕhovah," accessed February 21, 2018, https://www.blueletterbible.org/lang/lexicon/lexicon.cfm?t=kjv&strongs=h3068.
5. Prof. Jan Assmann and Dr. Rabbi Zev Farber, "Sacrificing a Lamb in Egypt," TheTorah.com, accessed February 21, 2018, http://thetorah.com/sacrificing-a-lamb-in-egypt/.
6. RJS, "The accuser is not Satan (RJS)," Patheos, November 6, 2012, http://www.patheos.com/blogs/jesuscreed/2012/11/06/the-accuser-is-not-satan-rjs/. See also, Tremper Longman III and David E. Garland, eds., *The Expositor's Bible Commentary: 1 Chronicles–Job*, vol. 4 (Grand Rapids, MI: Zondervan, 2010) 714.
7. Jack Wellman, "Who Were the Philistines in the Bible?," Patheos, May 18, 2015, http://www.patheos.com/blogs/christiancrier/2015/05/18/who-were-the-philistines-in-the-bible/.
8. Harvey E. Finley, "Gods and Goddesses, Pagan," Bible Study Tools, accessed February 17, 2018, https://www.biblestudytools.com/dictionaries/bakers-evangelical-dictionary/gods-and-goddesses-pagan.html.
9. Check out *The Book of Forgiving: The Fourfold Path for Healing Ourselves and the World* by Archbishop Desmond Tutu, a Nobel Peace

Prize winner and chair of the Truth and Reconciliation Commission in South Africa.

10. "Family Life: The Roman Empire in the First Century," PBS.org, accessed February 17, 2018, http://www.pbs.org/empires/romans /empire/family.html.

11. Carl Heinrich Cornill, "The Education of Children in Ancient Israel," *The Monist* 13, no. 1 (October, 1902): 1–23, https://www .jstor.org/stable/27899369?seq=1#page_scan_tab_contents.

12. Check out http://prisonbookprogram.org/resources/other-books-to -prisoners-programs/.

13. Julie Barrier, "What Did Jesus REALLY Write in the Sand?," Preach It, Teach It, accessed February 21, 2018, https://www.preachitteachit .org/articles/detail/what-did-jesus-really-write-in-the-sand/.

14. Bible Hub, s.v. "6886. Tsarephath," accessed February 21, 2018, http://biblehub.com/hebrew/6886.htm; Bible Hub, s.v. "6884. Tsaraph," accessed February 21, 2018, http://biblehub.com /hebrew/6884.htm.

15. Greg Lanier, "No, 'Saul' the Persecutor Did Not Become 'Paul' the Apostle," The Gospel Coalition, May 3, 2017, https://www.the gospelcoalition.org/article/no-saul-the-persecutor-did-not-become -paul-the-apostle/.

About the Author

Sarah M. Wells is an author, poet, essayist, and blogger. She serves as director of content marketing at Spire Advertising and as coeditor for the weekly column "Beautiful Things" in *River Teeth: A Journal of Nonfiction Narrative*. Sarah resides in Ashland, Ohio, with her husband, Brandon, and their three children, Lydia, Elvis, and Henry.

Web: sarahmariewells.com
Twitter: @sarah_wells
Facebook: facebook.com/smwells1982
Instagram: instagram.com/sarahmwells1982/

Help us get the word out!

Our Daily Bread Publishing exists to feed the soul with the Word of God.

If you appreciated this book, please let others know.

- Pick up another copy to give as a gift.
- Share a link to the book or mention it on social media.
- Write a review on your blog, on a bookseller's website, or at our own site (ourdailybreadpublishing.org).
- Recommend this book for your church, book club, or small group.

Connect with us:

🄵 @ourdailybread

🄾 @ourdailybread

🄱 @ourdailybread

Our Daily Bread Publishing
PO Box 3566
Grand Rapids, Michigan 49501 USA

✉ books@odb.org